Monsignor Patrick J. Corish (1921–2013) was born in Ballycullane, County Wexford. He was a priest in the Diocese of Ferns and was Professor of Modern History at St Patrick's College, Maynooth, where he also served as President of the College (1967–8). He was author of *The Irish Catholic Experience* (1985) and *Maynooth College: 1795–1995* (1995), was general editor and a contributor to the multi-authored series, *A History of Irish Catholicism,* and served as editor of *Archivium Hibernicum*, the journal of the Catholic Historical Society of Ireland. He also was a member of the Irish Manuscripts Commission (1949–2005), serving as chair 1973–6.

Interior of the Cathedral of the Most Holy Trinity, Waterford, the oldest Catholic cathedral in Ireland. Designed by architect John Roberts, who also designed the Church of Ireland cathedral in the city (completed 1780), Trinity was built in 1793.

The Catholic Community
in the
Seventeenth and Eighteenth
Centuries

PATRICK J. CORISH

ULSTER HISTORICAL FOUNDATION

ACKNOWLEDGEMENTS

Ulster Historical Foundation would like to acknowledge The Educational Company of Ireland (Edco) for permission to republish the original work in facsimile.

The Foundation also wishes to thank Prof. William J. Smyth for his considerable help in bringing this production to fruition; to Prof. Thomas O'Connor for his thoughtful and erudite introduction; and to Prof. Patrick J. Corish's literary executors, Catherine Farrelly and Msgr Hugh Connolly, for permission to republish the author's work. We are grateful for all the assistance provided.

FRONT COVER

Catholic church situated in the townland of Lisbane in the civil and Catholic parish of Ardkeen, Co. Down, courtesy of Fintan Mullan. Portrait of Primate Oliver Plunkett (1625–81), courtesy of the Pontifical Irish College, Rome. Extract from the Catholic parish register of Wexford, courtesy of the Diocese of Ferns and the Irish Family History Foundation.

BACK COVER

The Tryal and Condemnation of Dr Oliver Plunkett Titular Primate of Ireland for High Treason … (Dublin, 1681). The Tullymacnally Chalice and a small portable marble altar stone from penal times inscribed with interlinked IHS monogram and a cross, made so it could be easily transported to wherever Mass was being secretly celebrated, both items courtesy of St Malachy's College Archive and the Diocese of Down and Connor (see *Clergy of Down and Connor* (2020) for more information).

First published 1981 by Helicon Limited (The Educational Company of Ireland Limited) as part of the Helicon History of Ireland Series.

This edition published 2021 by Ulster Historical Foundation. www.ancestryireland.com

© Patrick J. Corish
ISBN 2021: 978-1-909556-95-9
ISBN 1981: 978-0-861670-64-2

COVER DESIGN AND REVISED LAYOUT
J.P. Morrison

PRINTED BY
Biddles Books Limited

Contents

The original Helicon History of Ireland series included the following titles:

Robin Frame	*Colonial Ireland, 1169–1369*
Art Cosgrove	*Late Medieval Ireland, 1370–1541*
Nicholas Canny	*From Reformation to Restoration: Ireland, 1534–1660*
Patrick J. Corish	*The Catholic Community in the Seventeenth and Eighteenth Centuries*
David Dickson	*New Foundations: Ireland, 1660–1800*
Donal McCartney	*The Dawning of Democracy: Ireland, 1800–1870*
Pauric Travers	*Settlements and Divisions: Ireland, 1870–1922*
Ronan Fanning	*Independent Ireland*
David Harkness	*Northern Ireland since 1920*

Deposition by 'Catherine' McTimpany naming persons attending mass [in Portaferry] *c.* 1671*

Catrin McTimpany being duly sworn upon
The holy Evanglist that she went in order to hear mass
Upon the 22^d of October & was too late And she also swears[?]
That the same[late?] people comming as if thy had been att mas[s]
And she further deposeth y^t [i.e. that] she went to mass upon the 17th of
July And heard the same performed & she also swears that
She hase been two Sundays at Mass after y^t time. She further
Swears y^t to the best of knowledge there was about 40
persons at Mass Patrick Oprey Priest. The peoples
Names that was att Mass

HER
Catrin McTimpan[y]
MARK

Meave McTimpany
Theophilus Pruin†
Arthur Carroll
Isbell Quin
Edmond Quin
Margret Savage
Cat Mcmulan
Rore McComora††
Hugh Ward
Pat Savage of Ballygalgett

†   [Prin/Burn/Bruin?]
†† [McConora?]

* Transcription of document used on the inside front cover. Courtesy of
the Deputy Keeper of the Records, Public Record Office of Northern
Ireland (PRONI, D552/B/4/2/1).

vii

Foreword

The growing interest in the history of Ireland in recent decades has led to a substantial increase in the number of scholars engaged in research and study. Old and cherished interpretations have been questioned, as historians discover new sources or ask new questions of the old. Much of this new thinking is, however, hidden from the public in learned journals, which are not easily accessible. The aim of this series (see page vi) is to make available to a wider readership the fruits of the most recent researches. Each volume is self-contained, and each author, a specialist in the field, has been free to put forward his own analysis of the period with which he deals. Taken together they form a lucid and stimulating account of Ireland's history from the earliest times.

Each author has also been asked to select a number of documents to illustrate his period. These will appear separately as the Helicon Documentary History and will, we hope, make available to a wider audience the basis upon which the study of our past rests.

Art Cosgrove
Elma Collins
GENERAL EDITORS

Preface

The Catholic Church has been a very important factor in the history of modern Ireland. The seventeenth and eighteenth centuries are in a very real sense the time when it took the form that made it such a weighty social force in the life of the nation. I trust therefore that a volume on this topic will not be out of place in the Helicon History of Ireland series.

When I first approached the topic I could find models in much work that has been done in Europe and more recently in England. As it took shape, however, I found that to evaluate the impact of tridentine Catholicism on the Catholic community I had to give rather more attention than I thought would have been necessary to the political and economic pressures that also shaped it. No doubt I should have anticipated this. Religion and politics are never very far apart in Ireland and there always seems to be an extra dimension in Irish history.

Within this community under pressure there were wide diversities of experience, diversities between one region and another and diversities between different social classes. The circumstances of its existence did not favour the keeping of records. In consequence, a complex story has to be pieced together from evidence usually no better than fragmentary. I hope I have succeeded at least to the extent of generating discussion.

Patrick J. Corish
ST PATRICK'S COLLEGE, MAYNOOTH

ix

Introduction

Patrick J. Corish
(1921–2013)

When Patrick J. Corish published *The Catholic Community in the Seventeenth and Eighteenth Centuries* in 1981, he was one of the best-known and most respected historians in the country. The author of a string of academic articles, the co-ordinator of *A History of Irish Catholicism*,[1] and editor of the sources journal *Archivium Hibernicum*,[2] and served on various historical committees, including the Irish Manuscripts Commission, which he chaired. He was also the head of a thriving history department in Maynooth. Some of the most promising PhDs in the National University were under his supervision, a number of whom would go on to join universities at home and abroad.

Behind these achievements lay a lifetime of dedicated service to teaching, to research and to Maynooth. P.J. Corish was a native of County Wexford and the scion of a family of Norman descent, a heritage of which he was enormously proud. Educated in the local national school and St Peter's College, he entered Maynooth in 1938, on the eve of World War II, commencing his studies for the priesthood as a student for the diocese of Ferns. Those were years of war-time privation. Hot on their heels would come the arctic winter of 1947, which remained etched on his memory like an icy inscription. His primary degree was in Latin and Greek; he went on to study theology and was ordained priest in 1945. He was a brilliant student and his Maynooth years provided him with a firm grounding in the classics, a familiarity with theology and a sound knowledge of scripture. Post-war conditions did not favour travel, obliging him to continue his studies in Maynooth. In 1947 he was awarded his doctorate in divinity for a thesis on the doctrine of the Fall in the Greek Fathers before Pelagianism. Soon afterwards he was appointed to Maynooth's chair of ecclesiastical history. In that role, he quickly distinguished himself as a conscientious and gifted teacher. Already as a young professor he had the force of presence and the style of delivery that would make him legendary in the lecture hall. Teaching across all years and on every historical period, he ranged widely, always keeping the big picture in view. Over the years he left his indelible mark on generations of Maynooth students, opening up for them the scriptural, theological and historical richness of their Christian heritage.

His approach set him apart from some of his older and more conservative faculty colleagues, engendering the odd academic rumble. His students, on the other hand, took to his pedagogy with gusto and appreciated both his intellectual range and his readiness to broach difficult questions. Many of them would later comment that they learned more dogmatic and moral theology in P.J. Corish's history course than in their dedicated dogma and moral classes. This was in large part due to Corish's knack of capturing the essential in a telling detail. At the core of his teaching and writing was the human subject in all its glory and tragedy. For those fortunate enough to sit at his feet his lectures were memorable experiences. Few left them unchanged. For the less engaged there was always enough to permit a decent stab at an examination question. To his more dedicated students he provided a peerless historical apprenticeship. For him, as for Aristotle, the unexamined life was not worth living.

When he took up his chair in 1947, the college was still a seminary in the Tridentine mould, a cloistered space, largely cut off from the outside world. True, students in the arts, sciences and philosophy followed courses approved by the National University of Ireland, of which Maynooth was then a recognized college, but overall the college was its own universe. In that scenario, history, like the rest of the arts and sciences, was regarded as the hand-maid of theology, relegated to a lowly place not only on the curriculum and also in the estimation of ambitious students. Perceptions of history would change under his leadership, in part because of his own impatience with traditional Maynooth pedagogy and the academic status quo in general. But larger factors were also at work, influences that occasioned a revolutionary shift in the way church history in general was taught in the universities. This was a shift that eventually engulfed Maynooth too, and one to which he would make a significant contribution.

Beginnings were inauspicious. In mid-twentieth century Maynooth, as elsewhere, church history was viewed as little more than a branch of apologetics, the means by which the various religious denominations born out of the Reformation, defended themselves and assailed their enemies. This began to change as church history was slowly transformed into an independent intellectual enterprise, one that attempted critically to understand the workings of religious communities and their interaction with and influence on society in general. This was part and parcel of a more fundamental reappraisal of the historians' craft, a re-evaluation that had its roots in mid-twentieth century Europe and owed much to the generation of historians led by Fernand Braudel (1902–85).[3] Their approach was characterised by a deeper appreciation of the human and the social dimensions of historical experience. This *histoire de mentalités* (history of mentalities) soon made inroads into traditional church history. Two of its most influential practitioners were France's Jean Delumeau (1923–2020)[4] and Britain's John Bossy (1933–2015).[5] Through their work, ecclesiastical or church history was transformed from an apologetically oriented account of the Church's theology and the clergy's activities into the flesh and blood story of the living Christian community, a community that was both heaven-bent and earth-bound.[6] P.J. Corish probably first got wind of these changes when reading for his MA in history in UCD. His MA subject, the seventeenth-century life and times of Bishop Nicholas French of Ferns, signalled a significant change in his historical focus. He turned his talents towards the effort to understand Irish Catholicism, not only in its doctrinal generality but also in its pastoral and historical specificity. In the course of the ensuing years, he joined Delumeau and Bossy as a gifted practitioner of the new history. He was also the key figure in introducing it, not only to generations of Maynooth students but also to Irish university history circles in general. Over decades of teaching, research supervision and publication, he made the new history his own, applying it sensitively to the complexities of the Irish religious experience. As he wrote himself, the 'basic question' was neither what the clergy were up to, nor the relationship between Church and State but rather concerned what was being achieved by the churches in the development of Christian life in concrete, lived situations.[7] This was the motivation for his undertaking and co-ordinating the multi-authored series *A History of Irish Catholicism*. A dozen volumes appeared and, although the project was never completed, it contributed to the renewal of church history in Ireland, inspiring a generation of new researchers. In the same vein P.J. Corish took up the editor of the sources journal

Archivium Hibernicum, a publication dedicated to making original sources in reliable, annotated versions, available to researchers and the general public. For him, the democratization of the means and methods of history writing was part of the new way of doing history and one of his abiding priorities. This work continued, when, after a short and unhappy period as president of St Patrick's College in 1967, he succeeded Cardinal Tomás Ó Fiaich (1923–90) as professor of modern history in Maynooth's NUI college. In that role he built on the work of his distinguished predecessor, making strategic new hires and building up the department's post-graduate cohort.

All of which helps to explain why, when he came in the late 1970s to write his own history of Irish Catholicism, it emerged not as an account of the institutional Church but rather as the story of a community's lived experience. This was the essence of his *The Catholic Community in the Seventeenth and Eighteenth Centuries* (1981), a masterful overview of the Reformation in Ireland and an exploration of why, uniquely in Europe, Ireland's rulers failed to win their subjects to their faith.[8] This well-received work was followed by the broader ranging *The Irish Catholic Experience: a historical survey* (1985), which remains the unignorable authority in the field today.[9] Both works are constructed around solid narratives illustrated with archival detail, designed to take the reader to the core of the experience in question. There is no danger of missing the wood for the trees: the author's attention to the particular is never at the cost of parochialism. Unafraid of the bigger questions that inevitably lurk beneath any attempt to live Christianity in the world, he also had the courage to articulate them. For instance, musing on the future of Irish Catholicism in 1985 he wrote, 'The Irish have only slender traditions of a philosophical humanism, much less of a secularist humanism. What humanism they are capable of is rather rooted in religion. It is in some ways a daunting thought that the real elements of pluralism in Ireland may well be the confessional churches.'[10] The intervening years have only served to confirm the sharpness of his insights.

A Maynooth man to the core, his dedication to the educational mission of the college, in theology, philosophy, the arts and the sciences was total and he gave in that measure. These professional concerns did not distract him from other important pursuits … like gardening. How typical of this warm, earthed man that the Junior Garden in St Patrick's College, whose guardianship he inherited, became his monument, one that continues to outfox the changes of history through the ceaseless renewal of nature, *exegi monumentum, aere perennius* ... .[11] In his later years, P.J. Corish remained a valued member of the *Catholic Historical Society of Ireland*, a key historical contributor to the cause of the Irish martyrs[12] and a friend to his old students. On retirement, in 1986, he accepted the formidable task of preparing the bicentennial history of St Patrick's College, Maynooth, which he duly completed in 1995.[13] In later years his colleagues and former students would meet him, at work, often on his knees, in his beloved Junior Garden or ambling around the college, ready to chat, delivering himself of the sort of lapidary remark that was his hallmark.[14] Right up to the end he remained completely who he was and even fooled some of his old students into believing that he would go on indefinitely. No one understood better than he the fallacy of that delusion. In January 2013 he was laid to rest in the cemetery of St Patrick's College, Maynooth, surrounded by many friends and beneath the shimmering copper beeches he had so long admired.

Thomas O'Connor
MAYNOOTH

1   See, for instance, *A History of Irish Catholicism*, [General Editor P.J. Corish], vol. ii, 5; *The Church in Gaelic Ireland: thirteenth to fifteenth centuries* [by] Canice Mooney (Dublin, 1969).

2   Archiviumhibernicum.ie.

3   Fernand Braudel, *La Méditerranée et le Monde Méditerranéen à l'époque de Philipe II* (Paris, 1949).

4   Jean Delumeau, *Le Catholicism entre Luther et Voltaire* (Paris, 1971).

5   John Bossy, 'The Counter-Reformation and the people of Catholic Europe', *Past and Present*, 47 (1970), pp 51–70; idem., 'The Counter-Reformation and the people of Catholic Ireland 1594–1641' in T.D. Williams (ed.), *Historical Studies* 8 (Dublin, 1971), pp 155–69.

6   Patrick J. Corish, 'The Catholic Community in the nineteenth century', *Archivium Hibernicum* 38 (1983), p. 32.

7   Patrick J. Corish, 'Irish Ecclesiastical History since 1950' in J. Lee (ed.), *Irish Historiography 1970–79* (Cork 1981), p. 171.

8   For a not uncritical review see, S.J. Connolly, 'Religion and History', *Irish Economic and Social History*, 10 (1983), pp 66–80.

9   For a review, see David Hempton, 'Irish Religion', *Irish Economic and Social History*, 13 (1986), pp 108–12.

10 Patrick J. Corish, *The Irish Catholic Experience: a historical survey* (Dublin, 1985), p. 258.

11 'I have raised a monument more lasting than bronze' (Horace, *Odes*, iii, 30, pp 1–4).

12 Patrick J. Corish and Benignus Millett OFM (eds), *The Beatified Irish Martyrs* (Dublin, 2005).

13 Patrick J. Corish, *Maynooth College 1795–1995* (Dublin, 1995).

14 Bill Cosgrave, 'Patrick Joseph Corish: priest and church historian (1921–2013)' in Salvador Ryan and John-Paul Sheridan (eds.), *We Remember Maynooth: A College Across Four Centuries* (Dublin, 2020), pp 433–6.

*for the students
who helped to get this book written*

1 Heritage and Challenge

I am not sure if I am ready to write this little book: indeed I am not sure if the book is ready to be written. Essentially, the theme concerns the development of a religious community, but political questions necessarily intrude, because at this period Irish Catholics came to be excluded from the general political community precisely because of the religion they professed. At two crucial points, therefore, political questions force themselves into the story, the point of exclusion and the point of readmission, and on neither occasion was religion the only issue. Here history is only following life. It has been well said that 'religious history' is an unreal abstraction from 'history', for religious communities cannot be separated from the many other political communities with which they intermingle, and the religious life of an individual does not exist in a compartment separate from his life as a whole. Traditionally, the history of religions has concentrated on one or other of two topics. The first is summed up in the phrase 'Church and State'. It is a real topic, and there is still much to be written on it, but it remains on the fringes of religious history properly so called. The second, somewhat less real, at least as it has often been studied, is a history of the clergy. It has too often consisted of a minute examination of clerical controversies, possibly because the surviving sources contain a disproportionate amount of material dealing with these issues. Quite often they are not of great importance in themselves; they must frequently have been quite obscure to the laity; and sometimes, it must be confessed, they did not have much to do with religion.

For a number of reasons religious history has been broadening its vision over the last generation or two. To begin with, there has been a new approach to historical studies in general, paralleling no doubt a shift in social consciousness, with an emphasis on social and economic history that has focused attention on the community itself rather than on its leaders. There has been a similar development within the Christian communions. For Catholics, this has been associated with the re-thinking of the idea of 'the Church' that led up to the Second Vatican Council and found expression in its decrees. Other Christian communions have had similar experiences. What is central to this development is the realisation that 'the Church' is not the same as 'the

1

clergy'. There are laity as well. As John Henry Newman put it at the high tide of nineteenth-century clericalism, 'the Church would look foolish without them'.

All this has led to a shift of emphasis in religious history. The fruits of the new developments in European scholarship are summed up in the German *Handbuch der Kirchengeschichte* (Freiburg 1965 ff.). Perhaps only in Germany could one continue to use the term 'handbook' for a work that fills more than two feet of shelf-space and is still not quite completed. Unfortunately, the very bulk of the enterprise led to the English translation being abandoned after three volumes had appeared. The whole work shows very clearly the present concern of church historians with the community, with daily Christian life and the impact of cultural factors and general social structures. A synopsis of the work of French historians of the 'sociological school' initiated by Gabriel Le Bras, and possibly a more immediate taste of the new historiography, is to be found in Jean Delumeau, *Catholicism between Luther and Voltaire: a new view of the Counter-reformation* (E. tr., London, 1977). It is fitting that the introduction to the English translation should be by John Bossy, whose own book, *The English Catholic Community, 1570–1850* (London, 1975) is a perceptive and pioneering study. My debt to these and similar works is not the kind of thing that can be acknowledged in detail: an appreciation, for instance, of how Professor Bossy can put new questions to what had begun to seem rather tired evidence in his essay on 'The Counter-reformation and the people of Catholic Ireland'.[1]

It will be obvious that in these new developments religious history is venturing into a difficult field. It is turning away from the well-documented, to the often secret life of 'the small folk who live among small things'. When the great positivist historians defined history, in Ranke's famous phrase, as *wie es eigentlich gewesen,* they insisted that such people could not be matter for history because with them it was impossible to find out 'what had really happened', and there is this much to their position, that it is indeed very hard to find out, or at least to be sure.

This is perhaps particularly true of the increasingly 'hidden' Catholicism of Ireland in the seventeenth and eighteenth centuries, the religion of a conquered people with scant past to keep for pride. Needless to say, this is an attempt at the story of one 'hidden Ireland' only: the other religious communities in the country also have a 'hidden' past to explore. Any exploration of Irish religious traditions can hardly hope to free itself altogether of the burdens of the present, in a country when the dead are neatly, however inadequately, labelled 'Catholic' and 'Protestant', and the ghosts of the present mingle their cries with the ghosts of the past. There is a natural temptation to turn one's back on this strand of Irish history, to say that in religious matters we have had too much history, most of it poisonous. This is a facile judgement. It is not peculiar to Ireland that historical enquiry should involve a link between the present and the past. Such a link is part of the very processes of history. Each generation puts its own questions to the past because as society keeps changing it develops preoccupations and approaches that differ from those of the preceding generation. That is the way the world is made and the way history is made.

A word on terminology. In Ireland there have been three main religious traditions, that historically have described themselves as Catholic, Protestant and Presbyterian (the Methodists do not really impinge on the period that concerns us here). Historically, when it was felt necessary to emphasise that Catholics were 'Roman' Catholics, the terms used – again in this period – were most often 'papist' or 'popish'. Again historically, the Church of Ireland has described itself as 'Protestant', though the terms 'Church of Ireland' or 'Established Church' have their uses when the emphasis is on its legal position, as the term 'Dissenter' has in the same context in regard to the Presbyterians.

The story opens about 1590, with the beginning of the effective mission of that central figure, the Counter-reformation Catholic priest, and closes in the early 1790s not so much because of the Emancipation Acts of 1792 and 1793 but rather because so many things came to a head in the last ten years of the eighteenth century that it calls for separate study. It may be that only a deeper investigation of what went before will allow us even to ask the right questions of this crucial decade. I confess I have been unable to refrain from trying to frame some questions, and even to suggest, very tentatively, the general shape of some answers.

Before there were Catholics and Protestants there were Christians. Despite the emphasis of the Reformation controversies, and doubtless despite the natural and professional temptations of scholars, it must be remembered that Christianity began, not with a book, but with a person. Jesus Christ did not put his teaching into writing. He inspired a small group to follow him. These in turn inspired others and the community grew into what soon came to describe itself as the Church. The Church soon produced writings that collectively came to be called the New Testament. Christians have always believed that these writings were in a class apart, and were written in the plans of God, but from the standpoint of history they appeared almost as it were by accident. The Person who appears in the faith of the Church and in these writings makes very great demands, that impinge nowhere more strikingly than in that very revolutionary manifesto that has come to be called 'the sermon on the mount'. A few may be singled out as central to the new demands of charity. The first is the emphasis that what counts is the interior disposition and not the external act, not even, in some way not even especially, the external ritual act. The second is the emphasis on how far the demands of charity now extend: that one must not resist evil, but rather return good for evil, and this not merely to those within the bounds of natural charity but also to those outside these bounds. We must love the enemy. Indeed, the real victory lies with him who can show that the final power is in powerlessness. To save your life you must lose it, even by death on a Cross.

This is truly 'the world turned upside down', difficult for men in any condition of life, but especially difficult for the warlike aristocratic kin-societies of medieval western Europe. Christianity would almost inevitably suffer some dilution if it were to exist in these societies at all. The problem was compounded by the fact that it had already suffered some dilution because of the circumstances in which it was preached to them. The first of them to accept Christianity, the Gothic peoples, had been attracted to it as part of the high civilisation of Rome, and had been converted as whole peoples rather than as the result of individual catechesis. These problems were aggravated when it came to the christianising of people definitely outside the bounds of the empire. The first of these were the Irish, and though the problems and procedures were to be formulated explicitly only by Pope Gregory the Great (590–604), specifically in connection with the conversion of the English, it is clear that similar circumstances had attended the preaching of Christianity in Ireland.

Gregory was a realist who had given much thought to the matter. He saw that these societies could not be changed all at once: Christianity would have to be grafted on to what was already there. Pre-Christian religious customs should not be so much abolished as, where possible, given a Christian form and content: 'for no one can doubt the impossibility of changing everything at once in rude and untrained minds, just as the person who sets out to climb the heights must do so step by step and not by leaps and bounds'.[2] Gregory could hardly have realised how slow the ascent would be, how long many practices, essentially pagan, would survive under a veneer of Christianity often thin enough, and how men and women would come to view the monastic state as affording the only possibility of being truly a Christian.

Here it is easy to be too censorious, to fail to make the effort of historical imagination enabling one to see a real Christianity co-existing with a real paganism, in, for example, such figures from early medieval Ireland as Fedlimid, the warlike king-abbot of Cashel, saluted in the Annals of Ulster on his death in 847 with the entry 'Fedlimid, king of Munster, best of the Irish, scribe and anchorite, entered into his rest', or to fail to notice, say, the very authentic Christian rule for the discernment of spirits occurring in the debris of debased myth, legend and folklore that makes up so much of the notes and glosses, of the eleventh century or later, to the *Félire* of Oengus:

> Once upon a time Moling was at prayers in his church and he saw a lad coming towards him, a goodly lad arrayed in purple raiment . . .
> 'Who art thou?' says Moling.
> 'I am Christ, son of God', says he.
> 'I know not that', says Moling. 'When Christ came to have speech with the Culdees, 'twas not in purple raiment or in kingly guise that he would come, but after the fashion of hapless men, as a leper or a man diseased'.[3]

It would be easy, too, to forget that it is a condition of the survival of Christianity that it exist in a living community, and to be over-dismissive of what might well be called 'civic religion', which allows the average sensual man, not perhaps the full implications of the Gospel, but at least to identify with the pieties of his kind and to cultivate an essentially religious sense of identity and loyalty that traditionally has brought the political bonus of providing the moral justification for the sacrifices that often have to be asked for if society is to hold together, and for which it may be hard to find a viable alternative.

It may be arguable that the Christian message can normally give to any society only a little more than what that society is disposed to receive. This raises the question of the role of the clergy, those who appear quite early in the Acts of the Apostles as especially set aside for 'preaching the word of God'. Here again controversy may have tended to obscure the fact that in the Christian message the word of God is a Person – or perhaps the very thought is so uncomfortable that the clergy in particular have been inclined to hide the Person behind the book. History argues powerfully that the quality of the Christian clergy has normally been closely linked with the quality of religion that society is capable of receiving, and it indicates all too strongly that there have been times when the clerical order has given it less than this. No doubt there have been individual exceptions within the clerical order, probably many of them, but these tend to leave only faint traces in the historical record. Clergy as well as laity found it hard to escape from paganism. What society demanded of its priests was that they be 'men of power' rather than good men, men of the Christian God. This development may be traced very clearly in, for example, the degeneration of the figure of St Patrick from the artless self-portrait of a holy, humble Christian in the *Confessio* to his depiction, in later lives, for example the *Vita Tripartita*, composed about the year 900, as a cross-tempered old man striding about the country threatening people if they do not accept his authority and pay him tribute. Patrick has become the figure of power, successor of the *draoi* and the *file*, and lesser clerical figures shared the same inheritance.

The fifteenth century is usually, and with a good deal of accuracy, painted as one of increasing religious problems, not just in Ireland but all over western Christendom. There were many reasons for this growing crisis, ranging from a decay in theology to serious problems in church-structures. Undoubtedly, the problems concerning the clergy must be regarded as central, if only because the high middle ages had placed on them so much of the responsibility for the general quality of Christian life; and because so much of this responsibility had been concentrated in the papacy the many problems of that institution were at the dead centre of the crisis. The clerical order had degenerated into a power-structure, and the benefices that had been instituted to provide the care of souls were now regarded primarily as sources of income that could be had by papal grace in return for payment of a fee.

Pluralism grew, and with it, necessarily, absenteeism. It is true that the obligation to provide for the care of souls was still legally imposed on the benefice-holder, but when he kept the law he did it as cheaply as possible and, therefore, inadequately. There was no shortage of priests, but most of them were an ill-educated clerical proletariat picking up a living as best they could as parochial vicars or Mass-priests. While the round of Christian life carried on it was seriously drained of content. A kind of anxious 'account-book' spirituality grew up, arising from a desire to be sure of standing well with a demanding God. This spirituality affected everything, even the central act of the Mass. The elaboration of the rite and the Latin language led to a kind of positive exclusion of participation by the congregation, and concentrated everything on what the priest did, regarded as having an almost magic efficacy. This efficacy was concentrated in the consecration and elevation, so that people rushed from one Mass to another to assist at as many elevations as they could. Popular piety devised new means of 'gazing at the Host', expositions and processions, especially on the feast of Corpus Christi, when the Eucharistic procession, in existence since the fourteenth century, became dominant in the popular devotion. Masses themselves were multiplied, with groups or fraternities each seeking its own Mass, indeed as many Masses as they could afford. Mass-priests multiplied, but the Mass decayed.

Instruction too was seriously deficient. At least in the numerous towns there was much preaching, possibly as a substitute for the instruction that should have come through the liturgy of the word but did not. However, these preachers by and large lacked sufficient instruction, and even the best of them were deficient in solid and central theology. There were vast deficiencies, too, in the catechesis of children, which the clergy had in practice left to parents and godparents.

Those who sought more than this thin fare tended to look for it outside church-structures, as in the movement known as the *devotio moderna*. Its most famous literary production, the deservedly enduring *Imitation of Christ,* has only two *dramatis personae,* Christ and the disciple, and its Eucharistic section is significantly headed: 'About the Blessed Sacrament'. The Christian humanists had essentially the same approach. Their model is Christ and the apostles. This model can be verified only by a study of the New Testament. There qualified scholars can make valid contributions; indeed when the Bible conflicts with ecclesiastical authority or scholastic theology the Bible must prevail. There was ground for the reservations of ecclesiastical authority, that there would be as many sects as there were scholars. The reservations of the humanists about ecclesiastical authority can be seen in the diatribe of Erasmus against Pope Julius II.

Turning to Ireland, we find the usual special Irish problems of local complexities and dearth of information. It may be useful to begin by underlining the distinction between the two cultures in the island. Gaelic Ireland was if anything developing its self-confidence. The Pale and the towns saw themselves as 'English', not perhaps English like England, if only because the elite had to come to some terms with the fact that the Pale had by now a sizeable Irish-speaking population, but 'English' none the less. What of the Gaelicised Norman lordships? 'More Irish than the Irish themselves'? Much ink has been spilled on the phrase, and the latest study makes some worthwhile points.[4] This way of speaking did not exist before the sixteenth century. The substance of the phrase, but not the phrase itself, occurs in a pejorative sense at the very end of that century and the beginning of the seventeenth, in writers like Spenser and Davies. The exact phrase, in a laudatory sense, comes quite late and is, essentially, associated with romanticism. In consequence, it may possibly be seriously misleading as a description of how people saw themselves in the fifteenth century. There certainly was enough to lead one to expect very full assimilation – intermarriage, the adoption of language, law, customs and dress – but it is necessary to be cautious. In a short but factually impressive study of the clergy of Connacht in the fifteenth century,[5] Ruth Dudley Edwards concludes that despite many assimilations to Gaelic ways the clergy of Norman stock had markedly retained many of their fundamental Norman qualities and much of their distinctive culture. In the pursuit of ecclesiastical office they showed themselves businesslike, acquisitive, avaricious, with administrative and organisational skills that clearly marked them off from their Gaelic neighbours. It should be recalled too that no historical situation is static. It does seem quite clear that at the beginning of the seventeenth century the descendants of the great majority of the settlers in Ireland in pre-Reformation times had firmly identified themselves as the 'Old English'. Perhaps the transition was not quite so great as the phrase 'more Irish than the Irish themselves' might suggest.

In Ireland as in western Europe generally the quality of the clergy suffered because of the system of papal provisions. The Irish clergy were great 'Rome-runners'. Their activities can be traced in detail in the published *Annates* and *Calendar of Papal Letters*. It is necessary to treat this evidence with some caution, for it is clear that in setting out their claims to Rome the petitioners were addicted to telling lies about their rivals, but when all allowances are made the picture is dark enough. The abuses got worse as the years went by. In 1533 Rory O'Shaughnessy, a layman who seems to have been illiterate, was appointed dean of Kilmacduagh. He never received orders, but was still dean in 1567 and doubtless until his death in 1569. In the diocese of Kilmore Cormac McGovern was appointed bishop in 1476. He had been prior of the Augustinian canons of Drumlane, Co. Cavan. His father, Thadeus, had also been prior there, and had been appointed bishop of Kilmore in 1455. In 1480 Thomas MacBrady was appointed bishop. He lived until 1511, and Cormac until the following year. For at least part of this time both were recognised as bishops of Kilmore, no doubt because each was so powerfully supported by his kin-group that he could not be dislodged: at provincial synods in 1492 and 1495 each signs as bishop of Kilmore. One can only speculate on what theological explanation of this unusual spiritual bigamy may have presented itself at the time, reflecting too on the fact that MacBrady, who seems to have won sole recognition in the end, is saluted in his obit in the Annals of the Four Masters as 'a luminous lamp that enlightened the laity and clergy by instruction and preaching'.

The case of Bishop McGovern indicates that transgressions of clerical celibacy were no bar to ecclesiastical advancement (Bishop MacBrady had a daughter Siobhán, who married Thomas, son of Cahal Óg MacManus Maguire, chief compiler of the Annals of Ulster). Cahal Óg, who died in 1498, had held many ecclesiastical offices, and had over a dozen children, some of them certainly born after he had acquired these offices. These same Annals salute him at his death, not only for his learning and hospitality, but as a gem of purity and a dove of chastity.

Again, we must try to probe the mind of the compiler. Canon law forbade the ordination of priests' sons, but a dispensation had become routine by the pontificate of John XXII (1316–34). Even more strongly, the law forbade the son of a priest to succeed to his father's benefice, but a way round this had been found by the time of Martin V (1417–31). All over the church clerical celibacy was widely disregarded. This development was particularly easily adapted to Irish kin-society, whose priests were regarded as one of the professional learned classes, and it seemed natural that the clerical office should run in families as the others did (in Europe generally, resentment against the married priest existed not precisely because he was married but because he expected to pass on his benefice to his son). One can see why Cahal Óg MacManus Maguire should have been honoured for his learning and his hospitality, qualities held in high respect, and also for having been a good family man.[6]

The monastic institute in Ireland was dying.[7] No other verdict is possible, even when everything in its favour is taken into account. Some spasmodic efforts at reform continued to be made, but the evils that affected it were too great. The root evils were wealth and the secularisation that was its consequence. The office of abbot was sought by younger sons of the magnates for the wealth it controlled. They were often freshly professed indeed, and sometimes not ordained. Often they did not reside. They were quite willing to change their monastic allegiance, from the Cistercian to the Augustinian, for example, if a richer abbey offered. Little distinguished them from their lay compeers except that they could not alienate the wealth of the abbey, but there were various expedients for turning it to personal profit, such as long leases with high entry-fines and low rents. It was only to be expected that numbers of them would take a concubine as their lay compeers took a wife (no doubt this is a charge to be treated with caution, but there are enough proven cases to show it was not uncommon). In Gaelic Ireland's kin-society the process of secularisation with all its consequences seems to have gone furthest. And everywhere there were dwindling communities, in the end rarely more than half a dozen, inevitably demoralised, and prone to follow the example of their abbots.

The case was different with the friars. With them there had been more effective reform-movements, and these had been particularly effective in Ireland. Interestingly, these reforms had first established themselves in Gaelic Ireland, and had spread from there to the English areas. There is plenty of evidence that in Ireland, by contrast with England, the Observant or reformed friar was a respected figure: 'the Observants, as they will be called most holiest, so that there remains more virtue in one of their coats and knotted girdles than ever was in Christ and his passion'[8] as a wrathful reformer wrote in 1538. They attracted those recruits who still felt a real call to the religious life, and trained them for what seems to have been an extensive pastoral mission. In the circumstances of Ireland, only a minority could get a university training, but their own schools – no doubt the *studia particularia* referred to in the *Calendar of Papal Letters* – provided a formation that may not have been academically theological, but certainly equipped them to preach and counsel. A surviving list of the more than a hundred works possessed by the Franciscan friary of Youghal in 1494, together with twenty-three added between 1494 and 1527, shows a working library of a community with no marked interest in theological study for its own sake, nor in the controversies beginning to blow up, but addicted to solid learning with a pastoral bent.

In this they were well ahead of the other pastoral clergy. The thirteenth century had concentrated clerical training in the universities. The results were not altogether happy, particularly because the older episcopal and monastic schools died out, and the clergy who were not university material might get little or no training at all. The results were particularly unhappy in Ireland, for no university was set up in the country, and a smaller than usual proportion of ordinands were able to make their way to Oxford or Cambridge or even further afield. It is clear that in Ireland some attended the schools of the friars, and there may have been other institutions or devices. But immediately before the Reformation the complaint is raised that those who seek education tend to study canon law to further their careers. The formation of a pastoral priest has low priority.

It is clear then that Ireland to a great extent shared the common pattern of a clergy who were not giving the laity more than they were disposed to receive and, in some respects at least, were giving less. Here the 'civic religion' that filled so much of the middle ages had an important role. For English Ireland it is possible only to catch glimpses of it, because sources hardly exist. Corpus Christi was a great festival day in Dublin, where the Eucharistic procession is first referred to in 1466. In the procession each guild presented the pageant for the mystery play it was its privilege to enact, and lists of these have survived from the end of the century. The plays as staged had pagan as well as Christian themes — 'the vintners acted Bacchus and his story, the carpenters that of Joseph and Mary'. One seemingly very popular entertainment with what may be described as a 'mixed' theme made its way into the Corpus Christi pageants, where 'the mayor of bullring, and bachelors of same' presented 'the nine worthies, riding worshipfully, with their followers accordingly'. The nine worthies, Joshua, David, Judas Maccabeus, Hector, Alexander, Julius Caesar, Arthur, Charlemagne and Godfrey of Bouillon, seem to have been a popular theme in Dublin and indeed elsewhere (the *genre* appears to survive in the 'mummers'). Kilkenny too had its pageants and plays: as late as 1637 the corporation paid ten shillings 'for copying the book of Corpus Christi plays'.[9]

Its enduring scribal tradition has left much more evidence for Gaelic Ireland.[10] In it we find many themes and usages common to western Christendom, but as a rule given a distinctively Irish bent. Here as in Europe the popular religious mind shows a mixture of Christianity and survivals from a pre-Christian past. God appears as a figure of power, power to reward but also to punish: heaven and hell are dressed out in elaborate mythological motifs. Christ is the divine hero who paid the *eric* or blood-fine for our redemption. With emphasis on his passion and death goes an emphasis on his birth and infancy, linked with devotion to Mary his mother. The saints too are divine heroes, dressed out in mythological motifs, figures of power, known to take vengeance, well worth claiming clientship from. One could never have enough insurance against judgement day. So, great chiefs elected to be buried in monastic cemeteries in the religious habit, first with the Cistercians, but in the fifteenth century with the friars, especially the Franciscans. When the last trump sounded it would be good to have a friar's hand to clasp.

This amalgam of paganism and Christianity runs through life. Both were real. Reliance on superstition, miracle and prophecy obscured but did not blot out the Christian quest for salvation. There was a strong Christian content to the ascetic exercises of fast and abstinence, even if there was sometimes a pagan one as well, when one person 'fasted against' another. The tradition of pilgrimage kept some of its ancient flavour of renunciation, and the great medieval work of charity to the poor, the sick and the pilgrim continued to be honoured. A general esteem of learning must have helped to raise the status of the clergy, who had always been counted with the learned classes, the *aes dána*. Society was quite capable of producing devotional literature in poetry and prose, though the prose was almost altogether translation.

Paganism and Christianity clashed particularly sharply in the institution of marriage, especially in Gaelic Ireland. It is perhaps pressing the evidence too far to say that in no other field of life 'was Ireland's apartness from the mainstream of Christian European society so marked' and that 'marriage remained in Ireland a purely secular affair',[11] for in Europe too the canon-law marriage faced problems of acceptance, and the Armagh registers, for example, show that numbers of Irish people were concerned that their marriages should be in accordance with canon law. However, many Irish marriages were not in accordance with it. In the eyes of the Church, marriage was a holy sacrament and Christian marriage was indissoluble, but it is all too clear that many Irish chieftains did not regard it as such. What would seem equally clear, however, is that remarriage on the scale some of them indulged in was possible only for powerful dynasts. What made many more Irish marriages invalid in the eyes of the Church was the wide range of invalidating impediments of kinship laid down by canon law, for in Irish society marriages were almost inevitably between fairly close kin. The medieval canon law did not require any outward ceremony, so that marriage would not have been invalid on this head alone. It was frequently canonically invalid, however, because it was within the forbidden degrees of kindred, and sometimes, especially with the magnates, because one or both of the parties was married already.

As long ago as 1927 Edmund Curtis noted that 'in literature as in all else, the native race of 1500 was taking the impress of a new, a Renaissance Europe'.[12] Some recent writing would indicate that this insight was true. For English Ireland, there is as usual a dearth of specifically cultural documents, but the cultural implications of some source-material that is primarily political is coming to be seen in a new light.[13] By mid-century the evidence for humanist influence in the Pale is clear enough. A generation earlier, pride of place must go to the treatise headed *State of Ireland and Plan for its Reformation.*[14] This treatise is undated and anonymous, but its date is close to 1515, and its author is a lay reformer of the Pale (there is good evidence that at this time and afterwards the clergy of the Pale were more conservative in their outlook). Brendan Bradshaw notes the specifically humanist approach, in the development of the idea of 'the commonwealth' and in the reliance on education to solve ills. Its approach to the problems of the Church is also decidedly humanist, in the emphasis on the need for a clergy both educated and devout, not, as they are, educating themselves solely in canon law for professional advancement:

> Some sayeth that the prelates of the Church and clergy is much cause of all the misorder of the land; for there is no archbishop, ne bishop, ne prior, parson, ne vicar, ne any other person of the Church, high or low, great or small, that useth to preach the word of God, saving the poor friars beggars; and where the word of God do cease, there can be no grace, and without the special grace of God this land may never be reformed; and by preaching and teaching of prelates of the Church, and by prayer and orison of the devout persons of the same, God useth always to grant his abundant grace; ergo, the Church, not using the premises, is much cause of all the said misorder of this land.
>
> Also the Church of this land use not to learn any other science but the law of canon, for covetice of lucre transitory; all other science, whereof grow none such lucre, the parsons of the Church doth despise . . .

For Gaelic Ireland, Curtis had already focused on Manus O'Donnell, chief of his name from 1537 until his death in 1563, and a recent study, entitled 'Manus "the Magnificent" ', fills out more detail,[15] though the comparison with Lorenzo implied in the title might suggest a similarity between the Swilly and the Arno greater than in fact existed. The signs of what might be described as Renaissance-type magnificence are clear enough, in, for example the lord deputy's account of Manus when they met in 1541, though it does not necessarily have its source in the Renaissance:

> At such time as he met with me he was in a coat of crimson velvet, with aiglets of gold twenty or thirty pair; over that a great double cloak of right crimson satin, guarded with black velvet, a bonnet with a feather set full of aiglets of gold . . .

On this occasion Manus showed an eye for the main chance that Irish chieftains did not need to learn from Renaissance statecraft:

> There is about him one that is a right sober young man, well learned, and
> hath been brought up in France, for whom the said O'Donnell desired me
> to write to your majesty, that it might please your majesty to give unto
> him a small bishopric that lieth in his country, called the bishopric of
> Elphinensis, in the province of Thomond . . .[16]

The traditional O'Donnell ambitions in Connacht had to be satisfied
by this young man, Conach O'Shiel, getting a royal nomination to
Elphin, whatever it was worth in that confused and contested diocese.
O'Donnell pressed his own luck too hard in seeking to be made earl of
Sligo.

What one senses in Manus O'Donnell is perhaps best described as a
self-confidence in opening up to new values while remaining firmly
grounded in the old. This appears in his statecraft, in his literary work,
both his poetry and the life he composed of his patron saint, Colmcille,
and in his relations with the Franciscans of Donegal, founded by his
house as an Observant community in 1474. At times they might suffer
from his witty but not really wounding repartee, like when he came on
Brother Hugh sleeping it off:[17]

> Bráthair bocht brúite ó fhíon –
> ná dúisgthear é gion gur chóir;
> gabh go ciuin ceannsa re a thaobh;
> leigtear d'Aodh an tsrann-sa go fóill,

but when the end came he, most naturally, was laid to rest 'in the burial
place of his ancestors at the Franciscan monastery at Donegal', as the
Annals of the Four Masters say, 'having gained the victory over the
world and the devil'.

As an example from the Norman lordships there might be cited the
poem composed by Richard Butler 'on the day he died':[18]

> Is áille Ísa iná 'n cruinne,
> is ná bláth róis nó lile;
> is tú bláth caomh ó Mhuire
> dochua a gnáthghael rinne . . .

'Richard Butler' cannot be identified. Robin Flower was 'tempted to
associate him' with a Richard Butler mentioned in 1537 in a document
in the Carew manuscripts, but there is no real basis for this
identification and on the whole it seems unlikely. The poem, however,

would certainly appear to be of the sixteenth century. Flower sees what he calls 'the Franciscan attitude' in the sincerity and spontaneity of the verse, but it is not impossible to see in it also the breath of humanism or of something akin to the *devotio moderna*.

This, then, was the Christian tradition that in the sixteenth century faced the prospect of becoming 'Catholic' or 'Protestant'. If in the fifteenth century the clergy had tended to give the laity less than they were disposed to receive, in the sixteenth, under the impetus of the Reformation, they set out to give them more. The Catholic reform derived from the Council of Trent, as developed and applied by the great reformers, the religious orders and the great bishops, the greatest and in many ways the pattern-setter being Charles Borromeo, archbishop of Milan (1560–84). Trent had inevitably left many things unfinished, but it had firmly established the shape of the Catholic reform. The key-figure was to be the diocesan bishop: all pastoral authority and all pastoral responsibility was concentrated in him. With him there was to be associated a worthy priesthood, mentally trained and morally disciplined in the new seminaries, ordered by the conciliar decree *Cum adolescentium aetas* in 1563.

In facing its massive problems Trent had concentrated on the clergy. Its one major decree for the laity, *Tametsi,* again in 1563, concerns the question of marriage.[19] The effect of this decree was to take the control of marriage out of 'civic religion', away from the kin-group, and to place it firmly in the control of the Church's ministry. This it did, essentially, in two ways. Firstly, it insisted that the marriage contract was the free choice of the individual, and that this free choice could not be invalidated by any undue social pressures. Secondly, it laid down what would for the future invalidate even such marriage consent. It would be invalid unless it was exchanged by the parties in the presence of the parish priest of both or either of them, or of a priest delegated by him or by the bishop, and of at least two witnesses. It was, very reasonably, provided that this decree was not to be binding in any parish until it had been duly promulgated there.

In other sacraments, too, there was a parallel stress on the importance of the spiritual choice of the individual rather than on any social implications. Baptism was to be administered as soon as possible after birth, with only one godparent, or at most one of either sex. The godparent was to be instructed in his or her religion to the satisfaction of the Church, and would normally be of an older generation, for the function of a godparent was the spiritual instruction of the newly-baptised, in contrast to what had long been seen in practice as the principal function of the many godparents, often little older than the child, of strengthening the natural kin-group. In the sacrament of penance, too, the heavier emphasis had hitherto been on the element of satisfaction, for it had been seen primarily as an instrument for settling quarrels and social feuds. Now the emphasis shifts to the element of contrition, with corresponding emphasis on individual repentance.

In this connection, moral theology took a 'casuistic' direction. The word has developed a pejorative sense, but in essence it meant that the new confessor must study 'cases of conscience' so as to be able to give prudent direction and judgement. In the same atmosphere the exposition of the faith, dogmatic theology, was normally described as 'controversies'. The old, easy-fitting 'civic religion' belonged to the past. Now to know the faith you had to know why you were a Catholic and not a Protestant. Formal instruction acquired a new importance. Here again Trent had established the pattern rather than filled out the detail. In particular, it had stressed the urgency of drawing up an official catechism, and this, the 'Roman catechism' or 'catechism of the Council of Trent', appeared in 1566. It was clearly designed for the clergy rather than for the laity. In it the humanist hopes in education were harnessed to the reform programme. Instruction was to be given by the parish priest, or in schools or confraternities under his direction or that of the bishop. Religion was to centre on the parish, the parish priest and the parish church, now to be a place for religious functions only, to the exclusion of many other functions it had sheltered in more easy-going pre-Reformation times. Other social forces were excluded or at least downgraded, notably the Christian household.

It will be clear that this far-reaching reform must have got under way only slowly, and that in particular it must have been slow in becoming the pattern of Catholic life. It was the pattern in northern Italy by 1600, mainly because of the impact of Charles Borromeo. In France at this date it was only beginning to take shape, because France had first to fight a long series of wars to decide if it was to be Catholic or Calvinist. It may then be expected that any full impact on Ireland will belong to the seventeenth century rather than to the sixteenth, not just because of geographical remoteness but also because of political and military considerations. Ireland was not unique in being a contested land in the second half of the sixteenth century. France had to fight its battles. There was a broad band of territory stretching from southern Germany to Poland that at first seemed headed for Protestantism but ended up Catholic. That this happened was in great measure because of the effectiveness of the Catholic mission, but its gains could hardly have been consolidated were it not for the fact that the political structures of the area ended up in the hands of committed Catholics. Here Ireland was quite unique. When the Tudor dynasty ended in 1603 the island had been militarily conquered, and the writ of a Protestant monarch ran everywhere, but the great majority of its people were, undoubtedly in some cases as yet implicitly rather than explicitly, committed to a religion which was not that of their civil ruler. The Ireland of later Tudor times was a very complex, not to say confused society, where people were only slowly and often painfully working out that they were Catholics, not Protestants. Recently there have been valuable new insights into this period, that now seem to be turning their attention to religious rather than more strictly political issues,[20] but their authors would no doubt be the first to admit that we are still some distance from a satisfactory synthesis.

In one other important respect Catholic Ireland at the beginning of the seventeenth century was unique. The general European pattern was of confessional states with religious minorities generally enjoying some measure of at least practical toleration. For the Catholic minorities in Protestant states the chief sign of their minority and tolerated status was that their Church was organised as a 'mission' without a diocesan episcopate. Quite early in the seventeenth century the Irish Catholic diocesan episcopate was re-established and succeeded in maintaining itself. Catholic Ireland had, not a mission, but a Church.

2   Not a Mission, but a Church

While structures are not the only element determining the character of a society, they are clearly an important element. It is necessary, therefore, to begin by considering the structures of the Irish Catholic Church. Roman reaction to the claim by Henry VIII and his successors to nominate the Irish bishops had been hesitant and uncertain. The report of the first Jesuit mission to Ireland in 1542 had not been encouraging. The second mission, that of David Wolf in 1560, had some success in introducing the reforms now receiving final shape at the Council of Trent and at this time being given effect by the Jesuits in other threatened areas of Europe. Roman policy on nominations to Irish episcopal sees was very hesitant. There was a temptation to name bishops when the political situation looked promising, for example, at the time of the Geraldine League in the late 1530s or with the Desmond revolt at the end of the 1570s. Overall, these Roman appointments faced increasing problems as the government of Elizabeth gradually extended its control.

Through Wolf faculties were issued to Catholic priests working in Ireland, giving them a canonical mission that in normal circumstances would have come from the diocesan bishop. This practice continued after Wolf's capture in 1567. Here there can be little doubt of the importance of the Observant friars, especially the Franciscans, though what details there are perhaps still await final evaluation. They had early emerged as a focus of opposition to the Reformation. Before it, they had been important especially in Gaelic Ireland, where they seem to have functioned among its kin-groups at least as a supplement to a necessarily untidy and probably ineffective parish system. They must have found the transition to an independent mission an easy one.

Towards the end of Elizabeth's reign new perspectives began to emerge. Some English statesmen, Francis Bacon for example, were coming to the conclusion that an element of religious toleration was a necessary ingredient in any solution to the Irish question. Pope Clement VIII (1592–1605) was prepared to explore a negotiated solution to the problem of Elizabeth's Catholic subjects, all the more as this would help the papacy to shake off Spanish control. The leaders who had up to this set the terms of the debate were dying: in 1594 Cardinal Allen, who had inspired the mission of the seminary priests to England but had later come to pin his hopes on a Spanish crusade to dethrone Elizabeth; Philip II of Spain in 1598; and finally, Elizabeth in 1603. The founding of Irish seminaries on the continent in the 1590s made available more priests trained in tridentine ways. In consequence of all these developments, vicars apostolic were appointed in considerable numbers in Ireland in the reign of James I.

The office of vicar apostolic had developed in the later middle ages as a Roman response to a situation where the nomination of a diocesan bishop was not possible because of a clash with the civil power. The device was to be used again when similar clashes arose with the absolutist Catholic monarchies of the *ancien régime*. It involved putting a person in charge of a diocese until the difficulties impeding the appointment of a bishop had been removed. One might expect some deviations from this pattern in Ireland at this time. What they were will appear most clearly from a comparison with what happened in two other countries with somewhat similar problems, namely England and the United Provinces.[1] Rome drew its information on all three principally through the internuncio in Brussels.

The United Provinces were to settle down with a sizeable Catholic minority under a Calvinist regime. Here Sashout Vosmeer emerges as the local ecclesiastical authority in the mid-1590s. He was consecrated a titular bishop in 1602, and given authority as vicar apostolic of Holland. This pattern continued through the seventeenth century. In England, on the other hand, disputes between secular and regular clergy led to the compromise of the appointment in 1598 of an 'archpriest' with authority over the secular clergy only. The disputes continued, and in 1625 a titular bishop was appointed as vicar apostolic over the whole English Catholic mission. This appointment solved nothing, and in 1631 his authority was so severely limited that he had to leave the country, and the Catholic Church in England remained without any definite organisation until 1685.

The Irish pattern was quite different. Appointments were made to the four archbishoprics, three of them at the instance of Hugh O'Neill. These, however, were exceptional. The pattern which developed was of nomination of vicars apostolic, not in episcopal orders, but to the historic episcopal sees. Some such nominations had been made in the reign of Elizabeth, but not so consistently as has sometimes been suggested.[2] There were three in the 1590s, but by about 1620 a clear pattern of vicars apostolic in each see is well on the way to being established.

At about the same date a further development appears – the replacement of the residential vicar apostolic by a residential bishop. This must reflect a Roman judgement that the Irish situation, which had earlier both required and allowed the provision of diocesan pastoral authority, was now ready for the presence of diocesan bishops. The point had been argued in Rome by Archbishop Peter Lombard of Armagh. A native of Waterford, he had been promoted to Armagh at O'Neill's request in 1601. After O'Neill's defeat he had turned to devising a working relationship between the Irish Catholics and King James I. By 1616, somewhat late in the day, he had refined a theory of the duty of Irish Catholics to accept James, not as their Christian king, which as a heretic he could not be, but as their lawful king, which he was, provided he ruled them justly, that is, repealed the penal laws. Four years earlier, in 1612, in a long memorandum to Pope Paul V, he had urged that bishops might very safely be nominated to Irish sees, provided they were men acceptable to the government and in no way associated with O'Neill.[3] His judgement was to be confirmed by such incidents as Lord Deputy Falkland's assurance conveyed to Bishop John Roche of Ferns shortly after his arrival in Ireland in 1629 that he was aware of the bishop's peaceable disposition and that as long as he gave no indication to the contrary he might rely on not being molested, or Wentworth's obviously friendly encounter with Archbishop Fleming of Dublin shortly after his arrival as lord deputy in 1633.[4]

The nomination of bishops in Ireland was further advanced by the establishment in the Roman Curia of the Congregation of Propaganda in 1622. A special Roman concern about the Church in mission countries can be traced back to the 1560s, and had developed especially in the pontificate of Clement VIII. This concern found final expression in the setting up of Propaganda. The new congregation had authority over Catholic affairs in all countries except where the Church was legally established. From the beginning, for reasons not altogether clear, it seems to have firmly backed the establishment of a diocesan episcopate in Ireland.

The first bishop to be named was David Rothe in 1618. A native of Kilkenny, he had returned to his diocese in 1609, as vicar apostolic, and also to exercise authority as Lombard's vicar general. Nominations came swiftly in the 1620s. By about 1630 each of the thirty Irish dioceses had its resident ecclesiastical authority – seventeen bishops and thirteen vicars apostolic, each committed to establishing within a territorial diocese the tridentine pattern of pastoral care, in competition, and as things turned out, largely successful competition, with the corresponding hierarchy of the legally Established Church. This situation was quite unique. In the United Provinces there was an organised Catholic mission, in England an unorganised one. In Ireland there was a Catholic Church. In an age when it was still accepted that Church and Commonwealth were co-extensive this posed problems indeed.

The first of these bishops were Old English. The Old English had pioneered the continental seminaries; they had been, very preponderantly, the first generation of seminary priests, and bishops from their ranks could more easily maintain themselves in Ireland among their kindred, as yet almost completely undespoiled of their property. Events of the mid-1620s, however, led to the appointment of Old Irish bishops in some numbers – the extension of the Counter-reformation mission in Ireland, the deterioration of relations between England and Spain, and the death of Lombard in Rome in 1625, where indeed his influence had already been waning for some time because of his unwillingness to return to Ireland. His successor in Armagh was an Old Irish Franciscan, Hugh MacCaghwell. Similar nominations followed rapidly, and there were soon two discernible groups in the hierarchy, on the one side Old Irish, mostly from the regular clergy, pinning their political hopes on Spain, and on the other Old English, from the diocesan clergy, in political matters hopeful of reaching some accommodation with the government.[5]

The first task of a tridentine episcopate was to provide a parish system of pastoral care. Post-Reformation Ireland had inherited the medieval parish system. This at its best had been untidy. Its origins lay in the twelfth-century ecclesiastical reform, as modified by the Norman invasion. The areas effectively penetrated by the Normans had developed small compact parishes, often corresponding to the feudal tenures in which the land had been parcelled out. In consequence, the right of presentation to a number of these parishes remained in the hands of laymen. In the Gaelic areas, pastoral care was for the most part supported by the hereditary church-lands. Their owners, the *coarbs* and the *erenaghs,* had become laymen, but retained their ecclesiastical functions. The *coarb* had more property, had greater stability because his property was assured of ecclesiastical immunity, and disposed of several churches. The *erenagh* had control of one church, and his right to ecclesiastical immunity for his property was not always recognised. Both *coarb* and *erenagh* had the right of presentation to their church-livings. They had the income from the property and a substantial portion of the tithe – half seems to have been the norm – from which they had to maintain the fabric of the church and pay dues and services to the bishop.[6] This territorially-organised system was not always adequate for the shifting patterns of Gaelic kin-society. The friars in particular seem to have developed a major pastoral role, at least to the extent of providing a ministry where no other was available. This role had become much more important during the fifteenth century, because of the many foundations of houses of the reformed or Observant friars, especially in Gaelic Ireland. Over the same period, the diocesan parish system was seriously eroded, more particularly in the non-Gaelic areas, by widespread impropriations of parishes by the monastic orders. All in all, the bishop was left with little voice in deciding who was to be the parish priest. For example, in the diocese of Cloyne in the fifteenth century, it has been estimated that of one hundred and thirty churches with pastoral care, seventy-five were impropriate to monastic or collegiate churches and twenty-one were in lay patronage, while in the Gaelic areas of the diocese a number were controlled by *coarb* and *erenagh* families.[7]

The Established Church was probably handicapped in organising its pastoral mission by being legal heir to this confusion. It won the decision that *coarb* and *erenagh* lands were to continue church-property, though it did not make good its claim to them all. The goods of the impropriated parishes were deemed monastic property. As such, they passed to the crown, and soon much was in the hands of laymen. The church buildings had been poorly maintained even before the Reformation. At the end of the turbulent sixteenth century by far the greater number were in ruins. The Church in consequence lacked material resources, and was heavily dependent on the extraction of tithe and other dues from a reluctant population. It also lacked human resources for its ministry. Very few ministers could be licensed to preach. The greater number were licensed as readers, that is, allowed only to read to their congregations what religious texts were available – substantially, in addition to the Book of Common Prayer, the New Testament and John Kearney's Catechism, printed in Dublin in 1571. Most of the preaching ministers were New English, that is, those who had come over from England since the Irish version of the 'Tudor revolution in government' of the 1530s, while among the readers were many of the 'old clergy', whose religious commitment was uncertain, even, one suspects, to themselves. In Cashel in 1615 the incumbents of two livings in lay patronage – one of the patrons is named as the earl of Ormond – are stated to be popish priests, while Corbally in Killaloe is reported as having its 'church and chancel up, but shut up against the minister and reserved for Mass'. These may be extreme examples, but they are in no way beyond credibility. At best, the ministry was in numbers insufficient to provide regular services even in those churches which were in repair. The quality of preaching was altogether inadequate, especially in the Irish language through which contact had to be made with the great bulk of the population. Trinity College began to provide a more credible ministry only very slowly and the situation did not really improve. The Established Church became more conscious of its position as a minority group, divided and insecure because of internal controversies, and faced with a growing strength of the competing Catholic organisation.[8]

If the mission of the Established Church was feeble, it would be a mistake to regard the success of the Catholic mission as in any way inevitable. It depended heavily on the numbers and quality of its ministers, the 'seminary priests' and the new or revitalised religious orders. These ministers in turn were in the first generation for the most part drawn from the 'inner Pale' and the towns, a community that styles itself 'the English of Irish birth' through the sixteenth century, but by the beginning of the seventeenth is distinguishing itself as 'Old English' in contrast to the more recent arrivals, the 'New English'.

The Tudor revolution was not exclusively concerned with religious change. It also represented a far-reaching political programme. Both concerns interacted. It is now agreed that at least notable spokesmen of the Old English element initially accepted the new programme as a whole with some enthusiasm, as a reform of Church and State in which they saw themselves as the natural leaders, representatives of a new humanist religion and statecraft presented with the opportunity of superseding outworn lay and clerical magnates. It is also agreed that these hopes had soured by the end of Elizabeth's reign. They were now religious 'recusants', unwilling to accept the Established Church. The transition was spread over the years, and we are still at the stage of informed debate as to when and why their hopes soured. Was it relatively early, and did it come about because the religious policy of the administration was forcing them further and faster than they were prepared to go? Or did it come relatively late in the century, the decisive elements being political and cultural rather than strictly religious, in the sense that they were gradually but inexorably excluded from the administration, and deserted the increasingly uncongenial English universities for the continental centres, where they slowly assimilated the Catholicism of the Counter-reformation?[9]

The question is subtle, the evidence fragmentary, and it would probably be a mistake to be too exclusive in our answers. There may be some danger of underestimating the religious element in the changing attitudes. From the reign of Edward VI, the Reformation had presented itself primarily as a new liturgy imposed by the authority of the king in parliament. It is therefore not surprising that conservative opposition should from the beginning have expressed itself as a preference for the old liturgy. In 1551 Archbishop Dowdall of Armagh, hitherto unquestioningly loyal to government policies, had taken his stand, that he 'would never be bishop where the holy Mass was abolished'. Bishop Bale's ham-fisted championing of the second Prayer Book can hardly be regarded as typical, but his aspersions on the reformed liturgy in Waterford as 'altogether used like a popish Mass, with the old apish toys of anti-Christ, in bowings and beckings, kneelings and knockings' foreshadow complaints that continue through the reign of Elizabeth that conforming beneficed ministers provided a liturgy as popish as they dared.[10]

It seems certain that in this reign active conformity made very slow progress indeed, and that though continuing examples can be adduced in the early seventeenth century, especially in Dublin and the planted areas, conformity was inclined to be short-lived unless it was part of a wider acculturation, or, to put it more crudely, a share in the spoils. At this time the Old English gentry and merchants were still propertied, but the political power that should have gone with property was being seriously eroded, and by the 1630s the property itself was under real threat. This political and social aspect of their problem was the most obvious one, but it would not have arisen in the stark form that it did had it not been for their religious recalcitrance.

Their political and social dilemma has been thoroughly studied,[11] and can be briefly summarised. Their strength was solidly based on land and commerce. The social group calling itself 'Old English', that at the time of the Reformation comprised only the inhabitants of the towns and the inner Pale, had now extended itself to include all the recusant gentry descended from settlers in pre-Reformation times. About 2,000 Old English Catholics in Leinster, Munster and Connacht held about a third of the most fertile land of Ireland. Dublin apart, the commerce of the towns was firmly in their hands. Ireland could not in practice be governed without their cooperation. They were nevertheless under continuing and relentless pressure. A rigorous insistence on the oath of supremacy finally excluded them from the central administration. The insistence could not be so rigorous at the level of local government, where through one device or another they maintained a strong position.

In 1613 they lost their majority in parliament, permanently, as things were to turn out. Within the structures of seventeenth-century parliament, this deprived them of the role of an effective opposition. Their property was endangered because their legal titles were in many cases shaky, and the demand of the oath of supremacy from an heir taking possession, though not consistently enforced, was always a hanging threat. Against all these perils their line of defence had been to invoke the royal prerogative, to appeal directly to the king. This was not altogether satisfactory, first in the face of James I's theological conviction that no papist could be a fully committed subject, and under Charles I in the face of Strafford's policy of regarding all papists as disloyal. In consequence, they turned to seeking legal parliamentary sanction for the graces they had up to this been content to enjoy by royal prerogative. Strafford brushed them aside. His detailed plan for a plantation in Connacht in 1635 was a turning-point. The Old English Catholics joined with the New English Protestants in the 1640 parliament in demands for the restoration of the legislative initiative to parliament and for the accountability of the executive. It was a desperate throw by a hard-pressed group, in view of their minority position in the Irish parliament, and in view of constitutional developments in England. Before the end of 1641 they had joined with the Old Irish Catholics who had had recourse to arms, not, they claimed, against the king, but in defence of their own threatened and eroded liberties. The confused decade of the 1640s may be regarded either as the end of one chapter or as the beginning of another. The political agreement between Old Irish and Old English Catholics was certainly a turning-point.

As already noted, the success of the Catholic mission depended on the supply of priests, regular and secular, 'new' priests trained for their ministry as Trent had laid down. This in turn demanded the establishment of seminaries to train them in Catholic Europe, for seminaries could not be set up in Ireland.[12] These Irish centres reflected the political fragmentation of the country, in that they were many, small, and in consequence often struggling to survive. Most of them came into existence because of initiatives by Catholics of Old English stock. The first was in 1592, at Salamanca. By 1612 there were four in Spain. In the Spanish Netherlands, Douai was established in 1594, and here too there were four foundations by 1610. The Irish college in Paris traces its origins to 1578, but it was only with the ending of the French wars that colleges could really be set up in that country. One came at Bordeaux in 1610, another at Rouen in 1612. The Irish college, Rome, came only in 1627. The Irish Franciscans set up Louvain in 1607, Rome in 1625. The Dominicans came to Louvain in 1626, while the mission of the Irish Capuchin Franciscans began with foundations at Lille in 1610 and Charleville in 1615.

It is not easy to arrive at even an informed guess as to how many students entered these small and scattered colleges or how many returned to Ireland as priests. A list drawn up in 1622 contains 222 names of priests who had been students of Douai college. Of these, 95 had entered religious orders, among them 40 Franciscans and 31 Jesuits. Between 1592 and 1629, 131 students for the Irish mission had been admitted to Salamanca. According to Archbishop Matthews of Dublin in a report in 1623 there were 800 secular priests working in Ireland, about 200 Franciscans, and about 100 from other religious orders. How many of these were 'new' priests? Again, even an informed guess is difficult to come by, but perhaps rather less than 30 per cent of the secular clergy, and of the Franciscans perhaps rather more than 30 per cent, may not be altogether wide of the mark. While the overall figure of 'new' priests among the secular clergy was rather less than 30 per cent there was a higher percentage among the Old English and a lower percentage among the Old Irish, because of the imbalance between the two groups in the first thirty years of the continental seminaries. By definition, all the forty Jesuits were 'new' priests. Their mission became very effective when about 1620 they succeeded in establishing 'residences' or houses where they could live a common life. They had good relations with the bishops, assisting them in their visitations and conducting diocesan retreats for priests. For the laity, they established schools, conducted catechesis, gave sermons, and administered the sacrament of penance to, it would appear, great numbers – though it should be noted that their mission to the laity was heavily concentrated in the towns. The Dominicans too, approximately forty in number, must as a group have been 'new' or Counter-reformation priests, because the order had been almost extinct in 1603, and had developed since then from a strong base of continental houses, mainly in Spain. These uncertain statistics would seem to suggest that overall there may have been a tendency among historians to exaggerate the role of the religious orders in the pastoral mission in early seventeenth-century Ireland, if only because the bulk of the surviving evidence concerns religious.

In Ireland, the Catholic Church had been committed to a tridentine pattern of pastoral care, based on the diocese and parish, with groups of parishes within the diocese entrusted to priests known as 'vicars forane' or 'rural deans'. It was probably no disadvantage that this pattern had to be established without reference to the existing parish system. Priests could be posted to areas of greater need as they became available, thus combining the flexibility of the mission with the pattern of the parish. There were, inevitably, counter-balancing disadvantages. Many priests were directly dependent for their maintenance on the wealthier Catholic laity, the landed gentry and the merchant and professional classes in the towns. This support of priests was part of a general mission of charity to the needy that of its nature is not easily documented. The chance that their sons became bishops has preserved in Roman archives the record of two women. Anastasia Strong of Waterford, mother of Archbishop Walsh of Cashel, kept open house for poor Catholics, giving them food and lodging, and gave shelter to all Catholics in need, at the risk of losing her property. This last remark strongly suggests that priests were among those Catholics in need. Of Joan Roche of New Ross, mother of Bishop John Roche of Ferns, it was explicitly stated that she kept open house for priests.[13] The priests simply could not have survived without this charity of the laity. However, this made them independent of the bishop to a degree hard to reconcile with the tridentine system. There is evidence also of continuing appointments being made in Rome over the heads of the bishops by officials of the Datary and the Secretariate of Briefs, the two offices of the Roman Curia which had controlled appointments to benefices before the Reformation. The biggest problem in establishing a parish system, however, arose from the difficulty in providing for the mission of the religious orders. This problem arose under two heads. One concerned the friars, the other the revived monastic order of the Cistercians.[14]

The Cistercians had had many abbeys in pre-Reformation Ireland. They seem to have died out altogether after the suppression, though a small community may have maintained a continuous existence around Holy Cross in Tipperary. A modest revival developed from the reform movement initiated at Clairvaux in 1615. Soon there was a small number of Cistercian monks in Ireland, claiming in title the abbeys of which they had been dispossessed. A serious pastoral problem arose when they pressed a claim to the many parishes which had been impropriated by these abbeys before the Reformation.

The problem with the friars arose because the Council of Trent had insisted that within his diocese all pastoral mission derived from the bishop. Religious were exempt from his authority only within their own houses. Even in their own churches, their mission as preachers and confessors to the laity was derived from the bishop. In Ireland there were few if any religious houses that could claim canonical exemption. Before the re-establishment of the diocesan and parish system the friars had ministered directly to the people on the strength of faculties granted by the Holy See. This ministry was incompatible with the diocesan and parish system envisaged by Trent.

The problem was intractable. Both friars and bishops had real fears. The friars feared that the bishops would gain a control over them far beyond that laid down by the general law of the Church, because conditions in Ireland did not allow them to set up houses fulfilling the legal requirements for exemption, and that they would be excluded from all pastoral work unless they were willing to become, in effect, diocesan clergy. The bishops for their part feared that unless the special faculties of the regular clergy were withdrawn many things the general law not merely conferred on them as rights but imposed on them as duties would be taken out of their control.

The battle was hard-fought and not altogether conclusive. At Rome, there was tension between Propaganda, favouring the bishops, and the Datary and the Holy Office, the respective sources of independent appointments and of independent faculties, favouring the Cistercians and the friars. In 1626 there was a Roman decision substantially in favour of the bishops. It was not easy to enforce in Ireland, and efforts to have it set aside continued, not without some success.

The available figures indicate that substantial progress had been made in setting up a parish system by the end of the 1630s.[15] Writing in 1637, Bishop Egan of Elphin, himself a Franciscan, reported that he now had forty-two parish priests, compared with thirteen when he had been appointed in 1625. In contrast, Bishop Roche of Ferns had twenty-eight in 1635, compared with 'more than thirty' six years before. The Augustinian bishop of Waterford, Patrick Comerford, reported in 1630 that his diocese had thirty-five parishes, forty diocesan priests and 'about forty' religious. In 1639 he had forty-five parishes, fifty-nine diocesan priests and forty-five religious – too many for the work to be done, he thought. Figures for five dioceses in the mid-1630s indicate that an adequate parish system had been established in areas with widely-differing needs and resources. Ardfert had fifty-two diocesan priests and forty-two religious: Tuam returned fifty-six parish priests, Killaloe forty-seven, and Kilmore and Kildare had each twenty-four.

Some estimate of the quality of these priests is possible. Even in the most favoured areas not all had had a seminary formation: in the less favoured, the 'new' priests must have been a fairly small minority. It would seem certain that the bishops, in their anxiety to develop the parish system, sometimes appointed less qualified diocesan clergy to the exclusion of better-qualified religious, though these, and the Franciscans in particular, had less-qualified in their ranks, and this problem was possibly aggravated by the fact that they had set up novitiates in Ireland, even though these probably improved in quality as time went on (for a few years in the late 1620s the Jesuits maintained an establishment in Back Lane in Dublin described as a 'university' by both friends and opponents). For the diocesan clergy, it proved possible to establish the institutions prescribed by Trent to keep them dutiful – annual episcopal visitation, regular deanery conferences, in some places annual diocesan conferences and retreats.

It is also possible to form some estimate of how much was effected. The picture of the parish priests of Elphin catechising every Sunday in 'remote woodland places' may be a little idealised, while the comments of Bishop Comerford of Waterford as early as 1631 may be a little acid. The clergy, he wrote, were undisciplined. There had been many apostates. The trouble was that they had too little to do. They seldom catechise and many of them are unable to do so. They say Mass in the morning, and then wander from house to house, 'playing or drinking or vagabonding': they 'live idle, sit among the best, go well clad, and if I would say it, swagger'.[16] The image is disturbingly close to that of the 'carrows' noted by, for example, Stanihurst, Spenser and Fynes Moryson, 'that wander up and down to gentlemen's houses, living only upon cards and dice'. Comerford is not the only person who refers to apostasies. Concern is expressed in Ireland and Rome because the Datary continues to grant dispensations for ordination to sons of priests. The sharpening quarrels between diocesan and regular clergy inevitably had a coarsening effect, and inevitably lowered the clergy in the estimation of the laity.

The laity could afford to be critical because they had taken their decision. Of this there can be no doubt at all. Indeed, if one accepts the testimony of bishops of the Established Church – Bishop Lyon of Cork Cloyne and Ross in 1607 for example, or Bishop Ram of Ferns in 1612 – the battle for religious allegiance was already lost at a very early stage of the new Catholic mission. Archbishop Bulkeley's detailed report on Dublin in 1630 shows sizeable Protestant congregations only in a few city parishes in the neighbourhood of the Castle. Elsewhere there is the same monotonous story – even where a service can be maintained the congregation is at best a handful, and in many parishes all the people are recusants and there is no service. The troubles in Dublin in 1629 which occasioned this report had revealed seven recusant aldermen and several recusant constables. The general task of presenting recusants was the responsibility of the churchwardens, but even close to the city of Dublin there were no churchwardens to present them. An English traveller, Sir William Brereton, found 'most of the inhabitants popishly affected' in Dundalk, Drogheda, Wexford and Waterford in 1635. His impression of Waterford tallies very closely with that presented by Bishop Comerford in a report in 1639.

Yet the attempts to enforce the recusancy laws more strictly in the reign of James I had brought real problems. Recusants singled out for particularly contumacious defiance, by refusing to take the oath of supremacy when elected to public office, or by failing to find a verdict for the crown when empanelled as jurors, were regularly brought before the prerogative Court of Castle Chamber. This was a fearsome instrument, for it was not bound by the legal procedures of the common law or by the scale of penalties imposed by statute law. The normal sentence was a crippling fine, at least £100 and sometimes more, and, as often as not, imprisonment during pleasure. Indeed, one prominent Dublin Catholic, Francis Taylor, died in prison in 1621 after seven years' incarceration, though in his case even the formality of Castle Chamber seems to have been dispensed with, for his name does not appear in its records. It does appear, however, on the official list of those whose cause has been put forward for beatification and canonisation as martyrs, as having given their lives for their religious convictions. With him are a number of others from the reign of James I. They include Cornelius O'Devany, bishop of Down and Connor, hanged in Dublin in 1612, whose name stands at the head of the list with that of the Elizabethan martyr, Archbishop Dermot O'Hurley of Cashel.

Pressures that might escalate rapidly lurked in the daily round of life. Certain categories were particularly vulnerable to the ordinary legal processes, suspected Catholic clergy, for example, or wards when they sued out livery on attaining their majority. But no one was really safe, for attendance at the services of the Established Church on Sundays was being widely demanded. The statutory penalties were substantial (a fine of twelve pence for each service not attended), but not crippling to a wealthy and determined recusant. However, the imposition of this fine might be only the beginning of his sorrows. Three refusals to attend service left him open to ecclesiastical excommunication, leading to a further fine or imprisonment or confiscation of property. It was not always easy to enforce the law in a society where Catholics still held so much property. The greater magnates were in practice too powerful to be molested, indeed powerful enough to protect others. Even where a process could be initiated by sworn information from a parishioner in default of a churchwarden the sheriff did not always find it easy to empanel a jury, and Catholic jurymen sometimes refused to convict, even though, as has been seen, they could be imprisoned for their refusal and sometimes were. It was small consolation that the authorities lacked the means, and sometimes the will, to keep a man imprisoned indefinitely. It may be accepted that particularly during times of sessions many Catholics lived in fear. The 'cases of conscience' on which they and their priests divided indicate what real misery was possible when the recusancy laws were enforced. If a Catholic imprisoned for failing to find a verdict against a recusant is offered freedom if he admits he had broken the law by so doing, may he accept freedom on these terms? Some said yes, others said he would be betraying his obligation to profess his faith. What of a Catholic imprisoned for refusing the oath of supremacy, offered freedom if he will ask for it 'with submission'? With submission to the law demanding the oath, or simply submissively? The counsel of the clergy was divided. For the imprisoned layman, it must have been tempting to try to count enough of them in his favour to add up to a 'probable opinion' on which he might in conscience act.[17]

Our most detailed information concerns the towns and their immediate surroundings, and it is very reasonable to assume that the level of conscious commitment declined the further one moved from them. Daniel (in religion Robert) O'Connell, one of the Capuchin co-authors of the *Commentarius Rinuccianius,* has left an engaging account of the activities of his kinsman, Richard O'Connell, who guided the affairs of the diocese of Kerry from his appointment as vicar about 1611. He notes in particular that he regularly attended fairs and public gatherings in all the towns of his diocese, especially Killarney, Castlemaine, Tralee and Ardfert, to make himself generally available to people, and also to try to curb drinking and fighting (the word he uses for fighting – *confusiones* – seems aptly descriptive).[18] It would seem to add up to the very rudiments of catechesis. Even in the towns and their surroundings, there are indications that the level of commitment was most conscious at the higher levels of society. In 1612 Bishop Ram of Ferns claimed that:[19]

for the poorer sort, some of them have not only discovered to me privately their dislike of popery and of the Mass, in regard they understood not what is said or done therein, but also groaned under the burden of the many priests in respect of the double tithes and offerings, the one paid by them unto us, and the other unto them. Being then demanded of me why they did not forsake the Mass, and come to our church, their answer hath been (which I know to be true in some) that if they should be of our religion, no popish merchant would employ them being sailors, no popish landlord would set them any lands being husbandmen, nor set them houses in tenantry being artificers.

The bishop's words give some indication that the Irishman has already learned not to tell the full truth to hostile authority, but one can accept that 'he knew it to be true in some' that fears for their livelihood kept them from conforming to the Established Church. The propertied papist could bear down on the poor man more heavily than the Protestant bishop.

Exceptional cases have to be left out of the calculations. There are passing references, for example, to such things as 'a popish schoolmaster kept to teach the principles of that religion' by a lay magnate in the Dublin area, but there is no means of telling how effective or how widespread this practice was. Neither can one estimate how much of the introspective and very contemporary spirituality of the writings of, say, Geoffrey Keating, came through in his sermons, and though there are indications that he was widely famed as a preacher it would be hard indeed to think of his peer among the diocesan clergy. Neither is it possible to estimate the extent of distribution or the effectiveness of the first Franciscan continental publications, Ó Maoilchonaire's *Sgáthán an Chrábhaidh* (1616), for example, or Mac Aingil's *Scáthán Shacramuint na hAithridhe* (1618).[20] Even at the highest levels of society, we have no real information on what books were read, or how widely. The success of the Catholic mission must be measured by the yardstick of the 'average' priest, with the minimum equipment his bishop required him to have, a catechism and a *Summa casuum conscientiae*.

With these distinctions in mind, namely that the level of personal commitment tends to decrease as one moves out from the towns and down the ranks of society, it is possible to attempt some assessment of the quality of religious observance under a number of heads: first, the parish and the Mass; second, what in ecclesiastical terms are the parochial sacraments and sacramentals, what the anthropologist calls 'the rites of passage' – baptism, marriage, burial; and third, the closely linked questions of catechesis and sacramental penance. Evidence of the survival of pre-Reformation practices, that have now come to be regarded as abuses, is to be found under these heads and incidentally elsewhere. Under all heads, the bulk of the evidence comes from clerical sources, particularly the bishops of both churches. For all the limitations of this evidence, however, it is possible to form some idea of the measure of success in building up a tridentine pattern of religious practice in Ireland.

This slant in the evidence may explain the emphasis on Mass-attendance. For the Catholic bishops, the church and with it the Mass was at the centre of the organised parish. For bishops of the Established Church, attendance at Mass showed the extent of failure to enforce the Act of Uniformity, and was the most striking measure of overall failure. With very few exceptions − one in the diocese of Killaloe has already been noted, and there are isolated examples elsewhere − the pre-Reformation churches, or rather those of them still standing, had been taken over by the Established Church. Where Catholics were still propertied, Mass was frequently said in the houses of the merchants and gentry. In many cases these also maintained the priest, and, rather ironically, in many cases also as the lay farmers of the local tithes they contributed much to the poverty of the Established Church. Where plantation had been extensive and propertied Catholics in consequence few, it would appear that Mass had to be said in sheds or out-houses or even in the open air. But already Catholics were beginning to build their own places of worship. They came to call them 'chapels': the title of 'church' was reserved for the Protestant building. The Protestants for their part disparagingly called them 'Mass-houses'. Both terms stuck. These chapels naturally varied in sophistication according to the standing of the local community, from, for example, the six Mass-houses erected by the London companies on their Derry estates before 1631 to the Jesuit chapel in Dublin, described by Brereton in 1635 (some years after it had been confiscated) in terms that at the same time suggest the general features of contemporary Jesuit church-architecture and look forward to the Catholic 'chapels' of the next two centuries, an occasional example of which still survives:[21]

> the pulpit in this church was richly adorned with pictures, and so was the high altar, which was advanced with steps, and railed out like cathedrals; upon either side thereof was there erected places for confession; no fastened seats were in the middle or body hereof, nor was there any chancel; but that it might be more capacious, there was a gallery erected on both sides and at the lower end.

Already by about 1630 there is a distinct impression of a community forming itself about the Mass. For the quality of this Mass-attendance there is no evidence, but from general contemporary practice and devotional literature it may be very confidently assumed that it was what today would be described as 'passive' — the congregation by saying its own private prayers associated itself with the priest at the altar who was performing what was essentially his business, not theirs.

This last consideration suggests that while the Mass was already a central mark of the Catholic community, the 'rites of passage' accompanying baptism, marriage and death may well have been more deeply rooted in the lives of its members. Legally, these rites fell within the competence of the Established Church, though it was not until the eighteenth century that civil law encroached on the common law principle that an exchange of marriage vows without any witnesses constituted a valid marriage. By the late 1630s — our detailed evidence is from Waterford, though there are enough supporting hints to allow the inference that it was the regular practice, certainly in the Old English areas — the practical compromise had been reached that Catholics wishing to get married sought a licence from the Protestant bishop, paying him a fee. They also paid a fee to the Protestant minister on the occasion of baptism, Easter communion or burial. They were then free to seek the rites of their own church.

Though Bishop Comerford in his acid letter of 1631 commented that 'women fondly esteem more the office of churching than baptising', the slight evidence which exists, in the form of synodal legislation, does not indicate any deep ecclesiastical concern about the sacrament of baptism. The point most stressed at the Drogheda and Kilkenny synods of 1614 was the limitation of the number of godparents — one, or at most one male and one female (Kilkenny), at most two male (Drogheda), with the implication that baptism is to be regarded as a sacrament of personal regeneration rather than as a social occasion for the strengthening of kin-groups. Neither does any serious concern in the matter of marriage appear in the episcopal legislation. The tridentine law as such is judged impracticable in Ireland, but marriage is to be celebrated before the parish priest and two or three witnesses where a parish has been constituted, elsewhere before a priest and two or three witnesses. The difference between marriage-vows and espousals is to be made very plain. There is to be diligent enquiry about impediments to marriage, normally by the publication of banns. If a dispensation is granted, care should be taken that the grant is susceptible of public proof. John Bossy registers the impression that in regulating marriage 'some progress was made', and this would appear so from some of the episcopal reports of the 1630s, in so far as these can be taken strictly at their face value.

Least progress seems to have been made in the matter of wakes and funerals, then, as before and afterwards, the religious rite most deeply embedded in Irish practice, and to some extent in consequence burdened with what can only be called a legacy of paganism. All cemeteries were in the hands of the Established Church. The Irish had traditionally preferred burial in monastic cemeteries. A cemetery, as its Irish name *reilg* indicates, was consecrated by the remains of the holy dead. When the last trump sounded, it would be good to claim clientship from neighbours as holy as possible. After the suppression of the monasteries, the monastic cemeteries continued to be sought as burial-places, and there was a long-established practice of making an offering for the rebuilding of the monastery on the occasion of a funeral.

Though Trent had not made parochial burial obligatory, it had insisted that a fee was payable to the parish priest if burial took place outside the parish cemetery. In Ireland, moreover, the bishops insisted that the regulars did not have houses that were canonically 'exempt places', and that in consequence the parish priest had the right to preside at a funeral even in the cemetery of a former monastery. Here were all the ingredients for disedifying public clerical squabbles, that no canon law could resolve, for there was no canon law to cover the quite exceptional conditions in Ireland. The clergy fought over dues and precedence, and competed to offer the laity what they wanted in the burial rites of the dead. In a long letter to Propaganda in 1632 the ecclesiastical authorities of the province of Cashel declared that it was almost impossible to find a lay person in Ireland who would wish to die without being clothed in the habit of some religious order. In consequence, though the funeral rites were held in private houses, the religious clergy normally presided at them, especially in the country districts, and claimed all the offerings made on the occasion of the funeral, allowing nothing for the diocesan clergy.[22]

In the matter of penance, the task of the reformers was to transform what had hitherto been seen primarily as a rite for the regulation of visible offences within feuding kin-groups into a sacrament of personal regeneration. Even the 'new' clergy had to work within the society they found. The Jesuit 'annual letter' of 1609[23] lays much emphasis on their work in ending social disputes. The bishops' reports are not so explicit in this matter, though John Lynch, their biographer, regularly includes the office of peacemaker among his stock attributes of a good bishop. It may well be that the bishops were afraid of accusations of involving themselves in secular affairs, but it may be too that they did so involve themselves more often than they were prepared to record in a written report that was always in danger of being intercepted. It might be noted that in 1642 they were appointed official 'pacifiers' of feuds among the confederate Catholics. It might be noted too that the bishop of Kilmore, who claimed in a report in 1629 that he had put an end to frequent divorces, and to disputes among clergy and laity, and had put down robbery and drunkenness, admits in a further report in 1634 that he had frequently been cited in the civil courts by clergy and laity who had taken offence, and that though he had refused to go his mission had been very much curtailed in consequence. The situation was not helped by the fact that the clergy were feuding so much among themselves.

The synodal decrees of 1614 leave no doubt that the penitential discipline they seek to impose is revolutionary. They speak sharply of a backward people and an ignorant clergy – *populi ruditas, sacerdotum ignorantia*. They insist that the penitent must have the rudiments of catechetical instruction; that what he is to confess is his own sins in number and kind, and not the sins of others. While the confessor must insist on restitution, he is to impose a light 'satisfaction', and above all not a penance involving monetary payments, and to remember that the imposition of public penance is reserved to the bishop.

What progress was made in this matter depended very much on the progress in catechesis. Here again it might be recalled that progress may be expected to be less as one moves out from the Pale and towns and down the ranks of society, into a people whose language was Irish, where less catechetical material was available than in English, possibly with a lower level of literacy and therefore more dependent on oral catechesis. As most of the people were Irish-speaking, and as the main centre of Irish studies was the Franciscan college of St Anthony at Louvain – nearly all the limited catechetical material printed in Irish originated with this community – the moves to limit the pastoral mission of the regular clergy cannot have helped its overall effectiveness. The synodal decrees of 1614 insist that all preachers must be approved by the bishop; those not approved must be content to teach the catechism. There was to be catechesis every Sunday, with a sermon where possible. Special attention was to be paid to the catechesis of children, to prepare them for first confession at the age of seven or eight, and for first communion at the age of twelve. The priest was to teach the rudiments – at least the Apostles' Creed, the Lord's Prayer, the Ave Maria – on every possible occasion, particularly in the houses in his parish which afforded him shelter. To some extent his efforts were supplemented by those of the schoolmaster, though he is a more elusive figure, and one might reasonably suspect that most of the schoolmasters who taught religion effectively were to be found in the towns or in the houses of the Catholic gentry. Parish missions, at this time being developed especially in France by St Vincent de Paul, were hampered in Ireland by the general untidiness of the parish organisation and the quarrels between the diocesan and regular clergy. Only the Jesuits seem to have kept sufficiently good relations to be able to develop this type of mission in any effective way.

The goals of the catechetical programme were modest, but the episcopal reports of the 1630s indicate that it had had a fair measure of success. Even Bishop Comerford, whose indictment in 1631 of the failure of the clergy has already been noted, reported in 1639 that in Waterford city both preaching and catechesis were the norm, and that in the country districts preaching was infrequent but catechesis more common; and though he still complained of an over-numerous and idle clergy he regarded the general progress as satisfactory.

There was still a lot of the old religion around, though it surfaces only incidentally and from sources which are hostile to it. A report in 1622 by a government official on the diocese of Meath, which had just got a bishop after a long vacancy, mentions 'Patrick O'Beglahan, anchorite of Fore, a pernicious fellow exercising ecclesiastical jurisdiction' – beyond doubt holding the position of '*coarb* of Feichin' (even more interestingly, this 'holy man in the stone' is still to the good in the 1680s, attracting hosts of pilgrims, and having had his cell rebuilt by Richard Nugent, earl of Westmeath, 'as a burying-place for himself and his successors').[24] In 1631 provincial statutes for Tuam order parish priests to hide away, and to note where they are hidden away, what are described in the veiled obscurity of Latin as *imagines obesae et aspectui ingratae* – in the vernacular, sheelanagigs. Pilgrimages were another occasion for episcopal concern. Pilgrimages to holy wells and trees are mentioned in the synodal statutes, and pilgrimages to the great traditional centres, such as Lough Derg, Croagh Patrick and Glendaloch, got new life in this period. The bishops' concern arose from the fact that these pilgrimages were the occasion for peddling much pre-tridentine religion, notably in claims made for indulgences and relics by the monks and friars – though one may express a doubt if the diocesan clergy were altogether blameless. Yet the bishops do not wish to see these pilgrimages abolished, but rather to eradicate the abuses connected with them.

The two things which seemed to have caused most concern to the bishops were sacramental penance and the rites of burial, especially wakes. There were many other social occasions, for the laity baptisms and marriages, for the clergy patronal feasts, where the bishops complained of excessive, indeed ruinous, expense on the provision of lavish food, drink and entertainment for the great crowds, clergy and laity, who were expected to come and came. It was not easy to change this practice, for it reflected a deeply-felt need to appear *flaithiúlach* in the eyes of one's peers. Indeed the indications would seem to be that the Old Irish in particular were with a reckless improvidence rapidly dissipating what wealth the plantations had left them because they could not adjust to a society where hereditary status was no longer impregnable and land was a marketable commodity.

Even in the towns the new religious commitment did not displace the old social habits. There is striking evidence of this from Cork city, where the Jesuits had established schools. Hitherto the boys of Cork had been instructed only in music, dancing and fencing: now they were given the moral and mental formation of the *ratio studiorum*. This led to a new level of religious practice not only among the boys themselves but also in their families. Long-standing feuds and hatreds were ended. Ignatius and Xavier became the popular Christian names in the city. The feasts of the two saints were kept with great solemnity, preceded by a fast and vigil. The feast-day itself was a public holiday, with all attending Mass, hearing a sermon and receiving communion. Then the clergy of the city were invited to dinner, and on these days none of them went without 'a sumptuous repast'. It is clear that the new religious practice has not displaced the old pattern of life.[25]

The gatherings for wakes caused special concern because in addition to the expense of the entertainment provided they presented aspects hard to reconcile with a Christian attitude to the great mystery of death. The traditional lamentation or 'keening' came in for constant criticism. So did the games and entertainments held in the wake-house in the very presence of the corpse: as the Drogheda synod of 1614 complained, 'through the evil of some idle fellows and jesters, there are bawdy songs, wanton mimes, and after dark filthier work of darkness'. Here again ecclesiastical disapproval made slight impact. The Church had been trying to christianise the rites of burial in Ireland from the very beginning. A few centuries of effort still lay ahead. Both the feasting and the sexual licence were too deeply embedded as an expression of the need to assert the continuation of life among the kin-group in the very presence of death.

The broad pattern of what the Church was trying to do at the beginning of the seventeenth century was, as Bossy put it, 'the enforcement of a code of religious observance in a frame of parochial uniformity', in place of the pattern of kinship groups with little real parochial structure, erratic in religious observance and sacramental practice. This represented a very radical challenge to much of the traditional social pattern. The Counter-reformation priest was every bit as revolutionary as the sheriff. Traditionally, the priest had been a man respected for his social position and especially for his power in relation to the unseen world. Now he has to be accepted as a man of religious learning and of good moral life, claiming authority in his task of forming these attributes in his parishioners. Externally, this authority was of necessity less obvious in Ireland than in the Catholic countries, but in so far as it was externally exercised it does not seem to have provoked any particular opposition. In 1614 the bishops claimed a right of general supervision, with power to inspect accounts, over the religious guilds and confraternities that had been fairly common in the towns. If problems arose, they have left no record. Problems did arise, however, when new clerically-controlled sodalities and confraternities were established. Predictably, the problems arose from competition for custom between diocesan and regular clergy and between different orders of regulars. The attempts to establish some parish system of poor relief probably made little progress. In the important matter of control over testamentary affairs, legally and traditionally an episcopal preserve, the bishops for the most part contented themselves with discreet pressure towards bequests in favour of the church with the threat of ecclesiastical censure against defaulting heirs.

To what extent did a genuine community emerge from all these developments? In Ireland, the very numbers of those involved must have provided very powerful support. It was not a question, as in England, of a small group finding cohesion in essentially domestic observances, especially in the cycle of feasts and fasts. In Ireland, the community appeared publicly as a community, fitting awkwardly into the commonwealth no doubt, but of necessity tolerated, and confident enough to make its profession public even in the immediate surroundings of Dublin. At Navan in 1622 it was complained that the Catholics had become 'so arrogant .... they carry a cross openly in the streets before the dead being carried to burial',[26] while for Drogheda the following year there is an account of high Mass and vespers on the feast of St Francis, attended by the whole town and by others who had come a long distance. Many of these no doubt were afterwards entertained to more material sustenance than the liturgy. The bishops several times expressed fears that too great a display of religious observance might draw down reprisals from the government. It did so at times, notably in Dublin in 1629, but in general the very numbers of the Catholics ensured a practical toleration.

'It is obvious', Professor Bossy writes, 'that the appearance of a separate, congregational register of baptisms marks an important concluding step in the process of separation'. The synods of 1614 and later years had ordered all parish priests to keep registers of baptisms, marriages and deaths. No such register survives from this period. It is possible that some were kept, though there are indications that priests were reluctant to keep them, fearing that they might prove incriminating evidence if things took a really bad turn (it has already been noted that the practice of Catholics registering their baptisms, marriages and deaths with the clergy of the Established Church seems to have been widespread). After the Restoration, a national synod of 1670 again ordered all parish priests to keep a register of baptisms and marriages. In Wexford town, these two registers begin in 1671 and are unbroken except for a short gap in the marriage-register after 1690.

To what extent was this Catholic Christian community the same among the Old English and the Old Irish? Bossy claims that with the appointment of Old Irish bishops in the later 1620s 'the tone of legislation about popular religious practice becomes a lot milder'. The evidence to support this view is very slender – in effect, the Tuam provincial synods of 1631 and 1639/40, which to me at any rate do not notably differ in tone from the earlier ones. Aidan Clarke would go so far as to say that to assert that both 'shared a common religion which pulled them together is to miss the point. The religion which they shared was not an agent of union, but a source of disagreement, and in practice the Church did not reconcile their differences'.[27] The continuing differences are undeniable but it might be closer to the facts to seek their cause, not in a differing character of the religious mission to each community, but in its inevitably slower penetration among the Old Irish, and even more in the political and cultural gap between them and the Old English. As the events of the 1640s were to show dramatically, the Old Irish had only an imperfect grasp of the delicate constitutional balances by which the Old English hoped to establish their position as good subjects of king and pope. It is also true that even those Old English ecclesiastics most favourably disposed to the Old Irish, who could come to feel that they too were the heirs of the traditions, saints and pilgrimages of Ireland's past, or who, long before Wentworth's plans to plant Connacht in the 1630s, could come to regard the plantations as in some sense a national calamity afflicting all Catholics, were still separated by a deep cultural divide, well exemplified in Bishop John Roche's ambivalent recommendation of the historian Geoffrey Keating to the historian Luke Wadding in 1631:[28]

> One Doctor Keating laboureth much in compiling Irish notes towards a history in Irish. The man is very studious, and yet I fear that if his work come ever to light it will need an amendment of ill-warranted narrations; he could help you to many curiosities of which you can make better use than himself. I have no interest in the man, for I never saw him, for he dwelleth in Munster.

Beyond question, as Aidan Clarke points out, the Counter-reformation gave the Old English a sense of identity with the religious cultures of Catholic Europe. They inclined to look especially to France as a model, not altogether apt as events were to show, of a religious community where the pope's rights were nicely balanced against the king's. While the Old Irish, for their part, did develop links in particular with the religious culture of Spain, it was among the Old English that there developed the sense of leadership in a new 'civility', 'a new plantation in religion' as the Jesuit Andrew Moroney wrote to his general in 1605.[29] Indeed by the 1630s one can see a religious vision among the Old English ecclesiastics which has fascinating parallels with the political vision inspiring their ancestors of a hundred years before at the parliament of 1541. Here these men had seen themselves as the natural leaders in bringing 'civility' to the whole of Ireland. Their hopes had been disappointed.

The 'civility' of the 1630s was tridentine Catholicism. How 'tridentine' was it? It should be clear that an affirmative answer to this question must carry some qualifications. In the judgement of an outside observer in the mid-1640s, the papal nuncio, Rinuccini, it was seriously deficient. It is true that Rinuccini was inclined to measure Irish problems by the yardstick of how things were done in the papal states, but he was in many ways a shrewd observer, and his judgement is supported by a report made by Bishop Dwyer of Limerick in 1649. The older bishops, Rinuccini wrote, had become accustomed to performing their functions in secret with the minimum of ceremonial. They did not wish to change, and would be content to have freedom to practise their religion quietly and secretly. The regular clergy he found even more lacking. They had grown used to lay dress and freedom of movement, and positively resisted any proposal that they should be subjected to conventual restraint, preferring to say Mass and perform other priestly functions in private houses, where 'often to our great scandal, on the very table from which the altar cloth has been just removed, playing cards or glasses of beer together with the food for dinner are at once laid'. This he found very disappointing after more than four years of Catholic political control. Some shrewdness in his comment must be admitted when he goes on to explain why things are so:

> It may be noted above all that this nation, perhaps more than any other in Europe, are negligent by nature, of all that might with industry and activity improve and mature them, but content themselves with great tranquillity of mind to what nature has given them with their earliest ideas, whence we find neither in ecclesiastical nor in secular affairs any solicitude or extraordinary diligence, still less any ardour tò promote the interests of the Church as there ought to be, and as little of anger when any attempt fails ... They have thus come to content themselves with a Mass in their cabins ... and quietly accommodate themselves to the misery of the times ... But this does not prevent them when instructed and placed in some post under strict rule from the first, from liking and pursuing the course they have adopted.[30]

And yet, as Bossy perceptively remarks, the 'Mass in the cabin' proved to have advantages Rinuccini could not have suspected. The strict tridentine pattern emerged in Catholic Europe, its religious exercises and in particular its catechesis solidly tied to the parish church, to the exclusion of domestic, household participation. This domestic participation was precisely the strength of the pattern established in Ireland, though the bishops had not sought it but merely tolerated it because they could not impose anything better. To Rinuccini in particular it was an intolerable situation, and he did his best to change it, but, as Bossy concludes, 'I think it was just as well for Irish Catholicism that he did not succeed'.[31] In the event, the untidy Irish system, with its strong emphasis on the home, proved more durable than the tidy continental system of parish catechesis centred on the church.

3   Between Two Worlds

On 23 October 1641 the Old Irish of Ulster rose in arms. By the beginning of December the Old English of the Pale had reluctantly agreed to make common cause with them. This agreement was not so much based on a perceived community of interests as brought about by outside pressure. Strafford's policies had been based on the assumption that all 'papists' were by definition disloyal, and they had gone a long way to producing the situation they assumed. Not that the Irish Catholics now in arms considered themselves disloyal. The Old Irish had explicitly declared that they were not in arms against the king, while loyalty was almost an obsession with the Old English, so long accustomed to toleration by appeal to the royal prerogative. In fact, the Irish Catholics at the end of 1641 were only one example among a number in the three kingdoms of Charles I of a sectional group who came together in a 'confederacy' to protect their interests not against the king but against his 'evil counsellors'.

By mid-1642 the confederate Catholics had set up an administration at Kilkenny.[1] From here, they exercised control over much of the island, with, however, important exceptions. The Ulster Presbyterians held Down, Antrim, much of Londonderry, and parts of Armagh. Dublin and the old Pale, and Cork with substantial territory around it, were held by the Protestants in the name of the king, though serious dissensions emerged among them as it came to war between king and parliament in England. The position of much of Connacht was quite uncertain because the marquis of Clanricard was very slow to declare his support for the Catholic confederacy.

The energies of the Catholics were directed to securing their position by negotiation with the king. These long, tortuous, and ultimately inconclusive discussions absorbed most of their energies. By contrast, the building up of their military forces took a second place. So did the strictly religious mission in the areas they controlled. They took over the churches, where they restored public Catholic worship. However, evidence has already been adduced to show that the efforts made to introduce a more fully 'tridentine' pattern of church organisation had only limited success, which seems to have been concentrated in the towns.

The course of these long negotiations does not concern us here, but the issues at stake do. By the end of 1642 the Catholics had formulated their basic demands. In matters of religion they were:

> That the Roman Catholic Church in Ireland shall and may have and enjoy the privileges and immunities according to the great charter, made and declared within the realm of England, in the ninth year of King Henry III, sometime king of England, and afterwards enacted and confirmed within this realm of Ireland. And that the common law of England, and all the statutes of force in this kingdom, which are not against the Roman Catholic religion . . . shall be observed throughout the whole kingdom . . .

This Irish Catholic version of a 'Petition of Right', seeking a return to 'the good old days', posed very thorny problems indeed. In the 'Great Charter' Henry III had declared:

> Firstly, we have granted to God, and by this present charter confirmed for us and our heirs for ever, that the Irish Church shall be free, and have all her rights entire and her liberties inviolable.

However, there was no agreement, right through the middle ages, on the 'rights and liberties' of the Church. In particular, the fourteenth century statutes which restricted papal control over the Church, if strictly invoked, would in fact have led to a schism. In practice, there had been a compromise. The weakened papacy of the fifteenth century had to agree to share ecclesiastical patronage and power with the king. The compromise had worked as long as the king had no interest in provoking a confrontation with the papacy. Even though the antipapal statutes had not been very effective in Ireland during the period immediately before the Reformation, when direct royal authority scarcely existed, after the Reformation it was not possible to consider any renewal of the practical compromise between king and pope within an agreed system. If the Church was to be 'free' more than the Reformation statutes would have to go. So would some of the pre-Reformation statute-law.

It would have to go because the king was not a Catholic, but the head of another Church and a personally committed member of it. Yet if it were to be repealed the Catholic Church would be left freer in relation to the state in Ireland than in any country in contemporary Europe. There were simply no precedents for any new structures that might be devised for the unique Irish situation.

During the long negotiations the irreconcilable interests emerged. The king would find it hard enough to maintain toleration by prerogative. To concede any more would alienate much Protestant support, more than enough to counterbalance any increase in strength resulting from an agreement with the Irish Catholics. It is true that as his fortunes declined in England he was prepared to take more risks in bidding for Irish Catholic support, but his viceroy in Ireland, the marquis of Ormond, appointed on 13 November 1643, felt constrained to maintain a harder line, conscious as he was that any concession to the Catholics would immediately lose the king the support of the Irish Protestants.

At the opposite pole stood John Baptist Rinuccini, archbishop of Fermo, who had arrived in Ireland as papal nuncio in 1645. He had come with instructions 'to restore and re-establish the public exercise of the Catholic religion in the island of Ireland'. His whole life had been spent in the papal states, and he simply did not have any real grasp of the appalling complexities of the Irish situation. Indeed, he would have had scant sympathy even for the compromise in Catholic France, where the king exercised considerable authority in Church affairs. For him, a restored Catholic Church in Ireland must in effect be an established Church, and certainly a Protestant king could exercise no authority over it.

The Irish Catholics divided. The Old Irish had little reservation in supporting Rinuccini. His programme in no way conflicted with their two main objectives, the reversal of the plantations and the restoration of the Catholic religion. They had never been deeply involved in the elaborate political compromises of the Old English Catholics. While they had declared their loyalty to the king, their natural leaders, soldiers and ecclesiastics, had been formed on the continent, in the world of Spain.

The Old English laity were easily driven into opposition to the nuncio. For them, everything must rest on an agreement with the king. They were desperately anxious for such an agreement because of the threat to their property, already developing under Strafford, and made actual by the Act for Adventurers, passed by the English parliament in 1642. This had arranged to pay for the reconquest of Ireland by the indiscriminate confiscation of all Catholic property. Faced with the unyielding stance of Ormond, they settled for a continuation of religious toleration by royal prerogative.

The Old English clergy were at the centre of these pressures. A settlement without an agreement with the king was unacceptable to them also. Like their lay kinsmen, they had a good appreciation of the constitutional problems and had grown used to a regime of practical compromise. On the other hand, their continental training had implanted in them a keen sense of the claims of the papacy. This meant that they could not settle for a mere continuation of prerogative toleration. In final desperation, a substantial number of them, including in the end twelve of the twenty-seven bishops, broke with Rinuccini in 1648, finding some support in the knowledge that in the Holy Roman Empire a peace unacceptable to the nuncio there was slowly grinding to a conclusion. They found Ormond as intractable as ever: he would undertake that the Catholics would not be disturbed in the peaceful possession of the churches they actually held until the king should declare his pleasure, but no more. A breakthrough came when news arrived in Kilkenny that the king was to be put on trial. On 19 January 1649 Ormond agreed to

> give unto the said Roman Catholics full assurance, that they or any of them shall not be molested in the possession of the churches and church-livings, or of the exercise of their respective jurisdictions as they now exercise the same, until such time as his majesty, upon a full consideration of the desires of the said Roman Catholics in a free parliament to be held in this kingdom, shall declare his further pleasure.

Although the undertaking was still conditional, by agreeing that the question of 'jurisdiction' would be considered Ormond had accepted the possibility of something going beyond toleration by prerogative. However, the king's trial opened in London the very next day, 20 January. He was executed on 30 January. Even had things gone otherwise, it is very doubtful if Charles would have granted the Irish Catholics what they sought. He had shown no concern for them in his final negotiations with the army and parliament, and these negotiations had finally broken on his stubborn defence of the position of the Established Church. For him and for Ormond the Anglican settlement was a religious as well as a political conviction.

The Irish Catholics, then, had not reached a satisfactory solution to their religious problem: indeed, the long years of negotiation had indicated that it was insoluble. Finally, by supporting the loser they lost their property which was the indispensable backing of their claims. 'Cromwell came over, and like a lightning passed through the land',[2] as Bishop Nicholas French of Ferns wrote sadly years later in exile. The war of conquest was followed by a land confiscation that in practice turned out to be a total confiscation of Catholic land. In consequence, the problem of being a Catholic in Ireland presents itself henceforth in a new context.

For the decade of the interregnum, there were to be no Catholics in Ireland.[3] 'I meddle not with any man's conscience', Cromwell had declared in 1649, 'but if by liberty of conscience you mean a right to exercise the Mass, I judge it best to use plain dealing, and to let you know, where the parliament of England have power, *that* will not be allowed'.[4] There can be no questioning Cromwell's sincere commitment to the difficult principle of liberty of conscience. Yet the government did exercise control over religious practice. 'Prelacy' as well as 'popery' was banned as contrary to scripture, and while in principle men were not compelled to attend religious services repugnant to conscience, penalties could be, and were, threatened for contumacious refusal to hear the word of God. Yet the regime, while it gave much consideration to the matter, never developed an effective programme for the religious future of the Irish now that they could no longer be papists. Indeed, in the judgement of its latest historian, T. C. Barnard, its attempts at evangelisation 'were totally inadequate and compared unfavourably with the efforts of the Church of Ireland'.[5] There was a deep-seated abhorrence of papists as a body, because they were not merely rebels but collectively guilty of Protestant blood. In consequence, there was a natural temptation to continue the policy of coercion. Plans for conversion divided on the issue as to whether conversion should include anglicisation, that is, whether or not the mission might be conducted through the Irish language. The number of ministers able to preach in Irish was completely inadequate. The only addition to religious books in Irish was a translation by Godfrey Daniel of *The Christian Doctrine* by William Perkins. Significantly, there was no Irish translation of the official *Directory* for public worship.

Nevertheless, Catholics did conform, and apparently in some but not significant numbers. In this matter, the reports of the authorities in the 1650s are confirmed by Catholic reports of reconversions in the early 1660s. Both sets of reports indicate clearly that those who conformed seldom if ever had a motive that might be described as religious. Catholics were subject to many compulsions. There is evidence that Cromwell personally gave some thought to the problems raised by the existence of a large population with no civil status at all. A query to the chief baron of the exchequer on 21 March 1656 explicitly asked in regard to Irish papists 'what privileges they may be deemed capable of'. In 1657, the Act for the Attainder of the Rebels of Ireland again raised the problem when it declared that all 'papists' and 'rebels' had been guilty of treason, but that this was now pardoned to those who had transplanted to Connacht. Very many had. If they were pardoned, what was their civil status? Not much, in the light of the Act for Discovering Papists of the previous year imposing an oath of abjuration of the distinctive tenets of popery. It had been opposed bitterly by Henry Cromwell, now in effective control in Ireland. That considerable pressure was brought to bear on Catholics under this act appears from a surviving presentment of recusants at Naas sessions on 12 September 1658. One hundred and nineteen named persons, almost all described as 'yeomen', were ordered to appear at Naas on 18 January 1659 to take the oath. None of them put in an appearance, but by this date the regime had begun to crumble.[6]

These last years saw another interesting development, in that, with the encouragement of Henry Cromwell, a political alliance was encouraged between the new planters and the 'old Protestants', that is, those who had secured estates under earlier plantations. Already by the Restoration in 1660 this alliance is coming to define itself as 'the Protestant interest'.[7] What is central to this interest is a determination to defend its title to the property it has acquired. So, just as the great changes between 1641 and 1660 led to changes in the problem of being a Catholic in Ireland, they also led to changes in the problem of being a Protestant. The new landed aristocracy, whatever its origins, by and large settled down in the Established Church. While it was still the Church of the nation in law, there was a change of attitude towards attempts to make it the Church of the nation in fact, that is, to convert the Irish Catholics as a body. This change of attitude may be discernible in a certain relaxation of pressure on the Catholics even before the end of the interregnum.

That pressure had been severe. The decision to ban 'popery' involved a total elimination of the Catholic clergy. While the war lasted, numbers of them were put to death, in indiscriminate massacres, as at Drogheda or Wexford, or by execution after capture. Yet even before it ended a more humane policy had emerged. Priests who undertook to leave the country were given facilities to do so. Perhaps a thousand in all went to Catholic Europe. Numbers of those who remained were rounded up and transported to the New World plantations. It is impossible to say how many managed to remain, but it was a minority, and during the worst years a small minority. When things began to improve towards the end of the decade there is evidence that priests began to return from Europe.

First hand reliable information on their ministry from Catholic sources is scanty. Inevitably, the parish system broke down, particularly where it was strongest, in the towns and among the Old English. Here the natural protectors of the clergy, the gentry and the merchants, were under orders to transplant to Connacht. All the sources agree in describing the ministry of the Catholic clergy as intermittent and extremely furtive. They could not turn to the laity for shelter and support, for this would have exposed their hosts to too much risk. They lived in huts in the bogs, in the woods, or on the mountains. They were probably safest in the towns, where some are known to have carried on a rather daring ministry under one disguise or another. However, as a general rule the priests moved about by night, saying Mass in some guarded retreat at or before daybreak. It was certainly in this decade that the tradition of the 'Mass-rock' stamped itself on the Irish experience. The set-back to the Catholic mission must have been considerable, even over the short span of less than ten years, particularly to the hard-won and still modest advances in catechesis.

Evidence allowing some assessment is available at the end of the decade. Archbishop O'Reilly of Armagh was in Ireland from October 1659 to April 1661, and made a number of reports on the state of the Church as he found it.[8] In a letter of July 1660 he listed the clergy in the ecclesiastical provinces of Armagh and Dublin: Ferns 8, Leighlin 4, Kildare 6, Dublin 7, Ossory more than 12; Meath 60 (this exceptionally high figure is confirmed by later statistics for this diocese), Armagh 26, Clogher 30, Kilmore 16, Dromore 12, Down and Connor 15, Derry 17, Raphoe 21, Clonmacnois 5. Other sources give at least fifteen in Killaloe in 1658 and thirty-two in Elphin in 1661. The numbers are perhaps higher than the national legend of Cromwellian ruthlessness might suggest, though priests are thin on the ground in the Dublin province, where the efforts to eradicate them had been most consistent. At best – with the notable exception of Meath – they are considerably less than half what they had been a decade before.

A stocktaking took place at provincial synods in Tuam (1658, 1660) Armagh (1660) and Cashel (1661).[9] These made it clear that the parish system was in great disarray, and the diocesan structure scarcely existed (the archbishop of Armagh and the bishop of Meath attended the northern synod, but there was no bishop present at the other two). Reading between the lines, we might deduce that things were rather better in Connacht, though even here there were problems, and worse in Munster, though it is a reasonable inference that they were worse still in Leinster, where it was not possible to convoke a synod at all.

The collapse of the parochial system had inevitably led to problems with 'the rites of passage', the parochial sacraments and sacramentals. Catholic parents – moved by fear, according to the Cashel synod – were bringing their children to Protestant ministers for baptism, sometimes after they had already had them baptised by a Catholic priest. The parish system of publishing banns, granting dispensations, and registering marriages had broken down. Marriages without any public record had inevitably increased. So, apparently, had marriages recorded only by civil law. A law of 1653 had set up a registrar in each parish, to publish the banns, either in the public meeting-house or in the market-place. The persons to be married were then to go through the prescribed form before a justice of the peace. They could also, if they so wished, have a religious ceremony, but not, of course, a 'popish' or 'prelatical' one. A register for the 'liberties of Cashel'[10] indicated that at least in the sparsely-populated areas registrars were given much larger territories than a single parish. This register covered much of Co. Tipperary and the marriages registered were almost all of Catholics. In a number of cases people had remarried, presuming the death of a partner who had disappeared in the great upheaval. For the first time the 'mixed marriage', between Catholic and Protestant, was presenting itself as a practical problem. Theologians were still debating if such marriages were allowable at all, but in practice a recognisably modern discipline was taking shape among Catholics. The bishop or diocesan authority was to decide in each case. If the marriage was permitted, it was a condition that it take place before a Catholic priest, that the Catholic party be allowed to practise his faith and that the children be brought up as Catholics.

At wakes and funerals the old problems were still there, and no new remedies were proposed for them. In fact, in this area things may not have worsened very much, if only because little progress had been made earlier in the century. At all social gatherings, whether they were family occasions such as christenings, weddings or funerals, or more public gatherings such as fairs, or 'patterns' or saints' patron days, it is clear that problems were raised by excessive drinking, that often led to disputes and fighting, especially at fairs. Drunkenness among the clergy was also a problem. It would appear to have given most concern in the province of Armagh.

It does seem beyond question that there had been a considerable growth in superstitious usages. It was perhaps only natural in times of such great strain. The synods set out these superstitions in great detail – invocation of the devil, witchcraft, a proliferation of dubious relics, curing prayers, holy wells (some of these apparently making a first appearance), pilgrimages and 'patterns'. The Tuam synod noted that certain laity, with pecuniary motives, had taken to going around with relics and imparting blessings. It also noted that James Finaghty, a priest of Elphin, was claiming to cure the sick with the relics of Archbishop Malachy O'Queely of Tuam, killed in 1645.

Two other points of interest might be noted here. The first is that the Cashel synod seems to regard the problem of usury as very serious: it describes it as 'intolerable', especially among the poor, and includes 'usurers' among a short list of public sinners. This probably reflects the breakdown of traditional society and also the introduction of money into the economy, though the synodal decree indicates that usury was a problem even when there was no money in question (it was practised both in money and in kind, *tam in numerato quam in fructificantibus*). The second point is that in both Armagh and Tuam it was felt necessary to issue a warning against Jansenism. In both synods it follows immediately after an injunction to parish priests to be diligent in catechesis. By this time Jansenism in France had developed into what was essentially a stern code of moral conduct. In its strictly theological aspect as a heresy concerning grace and justification it had recently suffered Roman condemnation. A number of distinguished Irish names had appeared among the supporters of the more theological aspects of Jansenism, but from now on anything that might be described as 'Jansenism' was to exercise only a very marginal influence on the Irish religious mentality. The turning-point may indeed have come during the decade of exile of the 1650s. It would seem, however, that some of the clergy now returning from France may have developed Jansenist leanings there. It was not to be one of the bigger problems in the future.[11]

The modest aims of the catechetical programme were restated. The Tuam synod lays down the basic books for the priest – the Bible, the Roman Catechism, the decrees of the Council of Trent, and a volume of *dominicales sermones* (this appears to be the first reference to the *prône,* or collection of prepared sermons, which was to be a steady standby in the years to come). There was to be preaching or catechesis for a quarter of an hour at public Masses, with penalties for priests who failed in this duty. Special attention was to be given to the catechesis of children, and to giving the ignorant that minimum instruction regarded as necessary for the sacrament of penance: as the synod of Cashel put it, many adults, even those of advanced years, were ignorant of the very basic truths of the Apostles' Creed, ignorant even of the Lord's Prayer, the precepts of God and of the Church, of the number and nature of the sacraments.

Improvements depended on the reconstruction of a system of pastoral care. Here the synods are on the whole optimistic. The Irish Catholics had high hopes at the Restoration. They felt their loyalty to the Stuart monarchy would receive its reward. The synods assume that bishops will be appointed and that the exiled clergy will return. They are particularly concerned with raising funds to send young men to the continental seminaries. Their optimism was at least partly misplaced.

Irish Catholic loyalty to the Stuarts was not well rewarded.[12] The king, whatever his intentions, was simply unable to fulfil any of the promises made by Ormond in the agreement made in January 1649, because the 'Protestant interest' held a monopoly of political and economic power, and meant to retain it. Only one Catholic was returned to parliament. The return was contested, and he never took his seat. Catholic peers in the Lords were in a minority. In these circumstances, all the forces of power and property could be used to back a propaganda campaign to show that all Catholics were necessarily disloyal in all circumstances. It is possible that the 'Protestant interest' was now to some extent coming to believe its own propaganda. In any case, the scene was set for an attempt by the king to satisfy all parties, which was sure to leave the Catholics, as the weaker party, the less satisfied. Their general prospects were not helped by the appointment of Ormond – a duke since 1661 – as lord lieutenant in 1662. He remained as implacably opposed to the Catholic claims as he had been in the 1640s, though on a more domestic level some Catholic Butlers were restored under his protection in Kilkenny and south Tipperary.

Desperate to prove their loyalty, a group of Catholic laymen drafted the formulary known as the Remonstrance in Dublin in December 1661. It consisted of a statement of grievances, a declaration of loyalty, and a petition for redress. Controversy centred on the second part, raising as it did the old problem of how to satisfy king and pope. The Catholic laity grew more desperate as the Act of Settlement in 1662 was suspended by the Act of Explanation in 1665. In consequence, the group of Catholic ecclesiastics assembled in Dublin in June 1666 was under very heavy pressure to endorse the Remonstrance. This they refused to do, but offered instead the first three of the six 'Sorbonne propositions' elaborated in Paris in 1663. These in fact conceded as much as the Remonstrance formula they had rejected, notably a denial of the pope's deposing power and an acceptance of the divine right of the king in temporal matters. The preference of the Irish ecclesiastics for the French formula must be explained by their desire to gain respectability in the eyes of their Church, though in papal eyes the gain in respectability was marginal. In any case, the first three Sorbonne propositions were not enough for Ormond. He demanded that the second three be accepted as well. These spelled out wide areas of 'mixed' jurisdiction where the French Church recognised royal rights. The Irish Catholic clergy refused to acknowledge that their Protestant king could have such rights. Gallicanism could never be acceptable to the papacy, but it might have to tolerate it in a Catholic country that was politically strong. There was no need to tolerate it in a politically weak Catholic community such as Ireland, nor indeed any possibility of tolerating what the Irish version had to be because the king was a Protestant.

So, the 1660s got no further in solving the problem of Catholic loyalty. In consequence, Catholics unable to appeal to special influence with, say, the king or Ormond, or not lucky enough to have had their claims processed before the passing of the Act of Explanation – these could expect only very limited success in regaining their property. Everything favoured the possessors – the earl of Essex called the land settlement 'a mere scramble ... the least done by way of orderly distribution of them as perhaps hath ever been known' and Sir William Petty compared the whole thing to a 'game or match ... the English have won and have ... a gamester's right at least to their estates'.[13] Overall, land in Catholic hands fell from 59 per cent to 22 per cent: in Connacht, from 80 per cent to 50 per cent, in Leinster and Munster from 66 per cent to 20 per cent, while in Ulster there remained only the earl of Antrim and a few other Catholic landowners.

Any assessment of the economic position of Catholics during the Restoration would be unbalanced unless account is taken of the emergence of large numbers of Catholics holding comfortable farms on advantageous terms. The process had begun under the Commonwealth, when there was acute need of people able and willing to work the land. It continued under the Restoration, and in these years of economic recovery it seems to have occurred on a large scale. For instance, Solomon Richards in 1682 and Robert Leigh of Rosegarland in 1684[14] are agreed that in the 'English baronies' of Wexford most of the old proprietors remained as tenants. In Leigh's words, they 'could not in the usurper's time keep their small freeholds, for all their strict observance of the old English customs, and so are now become tenants to those who had the land confirmed to them by the Act of Settlement'. For the north of Ireland, Archbishop Oliver Plunkett noted that these tenant farmers were well off, whereas the few surviving nobility, even the earl of Antrim, were sunk in debt, but he knew from within his own family how painful this process of coming down in the world could be. His own brother failed to recover the family property at Loughcrew in Co. Meath. Although he got a lease of a property at Ardpatrick in Co. Louth he seems to have been permanently marked by what he had to suffer. Shortly before his execution, the archbishop wrote from prison to his nephew Michael on 22 June 1681: 'You know that Ned is simple, and that by Cromwell's people what little land and mortgages he had left him by his father were lost'.[15] Mixed with these landlords come down in the world were men coming up in the world. These are even harder to track, but there must have been quite a number of them to explain the savagery with which they are attacked in *Pairlement Chloinne Tomáis*, the satiric poem which pursues them so venomously, and may well remain our principal witness to what must have been a fairly far-reaching social revolution.

During the interregnum special efforts had been made to clear all papists from the towns. These efforts had failed. The 'census of 1659' may be taken as giving the proportion of Catholics to Protestants with reasonable accuracy. It shows that Catholics form 60 per cent to 80 per cent of the town population at the end of the Commonwealth, with the notable exception of Dublin, where they are only 26 per cent. In the major cities, where 'town' and 'liberties' are distinguished, we find a higher percentage of Catholics in the poorer district, the 'liberties'. There are nevertheless sufficient indications that the town Catholics retained some wealth – in Galway, for example, where the Protestant infiltration had been particularly ineffective, or in Limerick, despite the fact that it was dominated by the earl of Orrery. Robert Leigh notes of New Ross in 1684 that 'the inhabitants are for the most part ancient natives of the town and country about it, and so are the chief merchants there that trade beyond seas, but those that have the government of the corporation and all public employments there are English of a late standing'. This distinction remained true of the towns generally, though in the relatively relaxed 1670s some Catholics were admitted as freemen in some towns – even in Limerick, notwithstanding the control exercised there by Orrery.

It was against this background that the mission of the Catholic Church had to be reconstructed. What toleration was enjoyed depended on the royal prerogative. Charles II was willing to be as generous as he dared, but the sharp ups and downs in his political fortunes resulted in sharp ups and downs in the Catholic position, all the more so as there was no longer an extensive Catholic propertied class to dampen the shocks. In the 1660s Ormond was lord lieutenant and the 'Protestant interest' was nervous. In consequence, there was steady pressure on the Catholics, enough to keep the clergy harassed but not enough to prevent their functioning. While the pressure was severe it was uneven – lighter in Connacht for example, or among Ormond's Catholic relatives, who included such great magnates as his brother Walter Butler of Kilcash. Some Protestant gentry are also noted for their kindness and consideration, even during the interregnum. Further, the pressure now took the form of an attempt to prevent Catholic rites of worship, or at least to make their performance as difficult as possible. It was a sign of changing attitudes that any attempt to enforce general conformity was virtually abandoned. Though it was not to be finally repealed until 1793, little will be heard of the Act of Uniformity after 1660. On 30 December 1670 Archbishop Oliver Plunkett reported to his agent in Rome:[16]

> The magistrates of the city of Armagh gave orders that all the Catholics of that town accompany them to the Protestant church every Sunday on pain of being fined half a *scudo* per person every time they missed. I had recourse to the president [the earl of Charlemont] against this decree: he ordered its revocation and gave instructions that neither priests nor lay Catholics were to be molested.

A mass-conversion of the papists had become economically undesirable. In these circumstances, practically all of the fairly considerable numbers who had abandoned the Catholic religion for one reason or another during the 1650s returned to it again. They are mentioned in thousands in the Catholic reports as 'converts', but they seem to have needed little evangelisation indeed. As was to be expected, the small number who had successfully kept their property by renouncing Catholicism did not return.

The Roman authorities reacted to the uncertain religious situation by delaying the appointment of bishops, while at the same time allowing the ordination of considerable numbers of priests with little or no intellectual or moral formation to fill the gaps left by the persecution of the 1650s. Both decisions had unfortunate results. Within a few years after 1669 the Catholic hierarchy was reconstituted. The early 1670s were more relaxed years. Ormond had been dismissed in 1669 and his successors were more tolerant. The general economic prosperity and a more relaxed and confident mood among the new landowners prompted

Petty to note in hope that increasing prosperity might stabilise what he described as the surprisingly good relations between Catholics and Protestants, though he did note also that a shared suffering was tending to unite Old English and Old Irish Catholics.

In 1660 it had been assumed that the Catholic church organisation of the beginning of the century would be speedily restored, but with only two bishops in the country and with toleration very precarious the parish system was not easily built up again. A proclamation of August 1660 had forbidden all meetings of 'papists, Presbyterians, Independents, Anabapists, Quakers and other fanatical persons', and though in the nature of things it was very hard to enforce it against papists and Presbyterians it did make meeting for worship an unlawful assembly. With diocesan authority so uncertain, the Catholic clergy had full scope for quarrelling among themselves over who had the right to what. It is quite hard to be certain what exactly was going on at pastoral level through the 1660s. For seven dioceses we have figures for the number of priests at the beginning of the decade and again at the end. In Raphoe there seems to have been a decline in numbers; in Elphin an increase from thirty-two to forty-four. Kildare, Leighlin, Kilfenora, Ossory and Down and Connor more than double their numbers over these ten years, but still have fewer than they had in the 1640s. The friars are also increasing in numbers, the Franciscans most of all, it would appear. However, it must be borne in mind that most of these additional priests were ordained in a hurry and with little or no preparation. Nor was a seminary training any guarantee against reversion. Terence O'Kelly had been one of the first students of the Irish college, Rome, in the 1620s. Even then he had been a troublemaker. Yet he succeeded in getting himself named vicar apostolic of his native diocese of Derry in 1629. The diocese was deeply involved in the Ulster plantation, and no bishop was appointed there even in the 1640s. The Roman authorities heard little from Terence O'Kelly, but in the 1660s they several times got disturbing news of him from others. In 1669 he was reported as having lived in public concubinage for twenty-two years, a scandal to Catholic and Protestant alike. Several attempts were made to remove this seminary-trained relic of the past, but he held on, not despising judiciously-chosen appeals to the civil authorities, until, in his own words, he was 'unhorsed' by the 'Roman primate', Oliver Plunkett.

A report of his work in the diocese of Achonry, by a priest named John Sullivan, and dated 3 March 1668, will help to add to the impressionistic picture which is all that can be expected of the 1660s.

His matter-of-fact presentation compels acceptance of what he says (it is corroborated by the provincial synods at the beginning of the decade). Others may tell you differently, he says, and they may well be in fact recounting their experiences, for there are wide differences as between region and region and as between class and class: all he claims to do is to recount his own experience. His problems arose when people with little if any instruction approached him for absolution: indeed, he said, many Catholics, even those prepared to suffer for their faith, thought it enough if they attended Mass. They told him that there were three gods, four gods even – the Father, the Son, the Holy Ghost and the Blessed Virgin (some added the names of apostles and other saints). The Father became man, the three persons became man. A favourite oath was to swear 'by the seven all-powerful persons of the Trinity', which seems to indicate a certain confusion between the number of the divine persons and the number of the sacraments. He would not absolve such people, but some priests did, some through ignorance, some through greed. Sullivan notes the great scarcity of priests, but it does not appear to have struck him that some priests might have given absolution in these cases precisely because it might be a long time before a priest came round again, nor does he appear to have felt that there was a case to answer when one penitent met his questioning by saying that these were subtle matters and quite beyond him: all he wanted was forgiveness for his sins.[17]

Sullivan is witness to the fact that the state of affairs he describes shows things at their worst and that they were often better. This is confirmed by the earliest reports of the newly appointed bishops at the beginning of the 1670s. The first appointments came at the beginning of 1669, and by the end of 1671 nearly every diocese had its bishop or vicar general: it was clear who was in charge. These new church authorities, like those appointed at the beginning of the century, included a number of highly capable men and some very attractive personalities. Archbishop Oliver Plunkett of Armagh is the best known of them, more for his heroic and saintly death than for his dedicated but in some respects contentious life. Archbishop Peter Talbot of Dublin is less fortunate, in that his disputes with the archbishop of Armagh tend to be better remembered than his lonely death in prison during the Popish Plot. The government regarded Bishop John O'Moloney of Killaloe as in many respects the most capable of them all. Two might be singled out to represent the attractive personalities – John Brenan, bishop of Waterford and later archbishop of Cashel, many times having to act as peacemaker, and Luke Wadding, bishop of Ferns, whose personality is revealed in the surviving sources more clearly than those of his colleagues.

These bishops were starting their rebuilding pretty well from the foundations. The rebuilding of the shattered parish system had been very slow in the absence of a clear diocesan authority. This lack of authority had encouraged clerical dissension, regular against diocesan and regulars and diocesans between themselves. These dissensions had been encouraged by civil authority. Many of the quarrelling clergy were ill-equipped for even rudimentary catechesis, and it may be taken as certain that in this crucial matter the modest successes of the first half of the century had not been maintained.

The bishops had the familiar remedies for familiar disorders. Their diocesan mission is to rest on a system of parish ministration. At its centre will be the Mass of obligation: the thatched Mass-house now establishes itself as the rule in the country districts of the south. There will still be widespread exceptions, where the landlord will not allow a Mass-house, and in the north of the country Mass in the open air will be by far the more common for a full century to come. In the towns the Mass-house will often be a more substantial building, and here and there it may have some pretensions to dignity, but even mud and thatch is a sign of poverty rather than of misery, and Irish Catholics are learning that it may be good policy in matters of religion to appear a little poorer than they really are. The widespread toleration of the Mass-house is a further indication that the Established Church was tacitly abandoning a missionary role. The Catholic ministry comes to be more and more tolerated as a fact of life – the Sunday Mass, the 'parish sacraments' or 'rites of passage', the attempt to ensure that the clergy are able to impart basic catechesis and that they do in fact impart it.

In pre-industrial England social stability was provided within a general framework of parson, squire and parish. It will be apparent that no such stability might be expected from the system now emerging in Ireland. In the preceding chapter it has been pointed out that the parish system Ireland inherited from the middle ages needed drastic reconstruction. This it did not get. The detailed surveys made in connection with the confiscations of the 1650s had given the administration a reasonably exact knowledge of parish boundaries, and this knowledge only confirmed the need for reorganisation. The administration of the interregnum planned reorganisation, but never got round to it. An Act of 1662 allowed the chief governor to unite or divide parishes, but he had to seek the consent of so many interests that little could be done, and the existing system remained substantially unaltered.

Over most of the country, the adherents of the Established Church were too few in number to work these parishes as an ecclesiastical system. As active citizenship came to be confined in practice to the members of the Established Church the parishes proved too numerous and in many cases too small to serve as units of local civil administration, though the fact that they came to be known as 'civil parishes' may afford some indication, for what it is worth, that their civil role was somewhat more effective than their ecclesiastical one. The ecclesiastical parishes of the Catholic majority had no necessary relation to the pre-reformation parish divisions, though attempts were made, with lasting success in many cases, to adapt the developing Catholic mission to unions of already existing parishes.

A pattern is emerging in Catholic Ireland. It might perhaps be more forcefully described as a lack of a pattern. What is lacking is an overall framework, what was provided in England by the parish, the squire and the parson. In contrast, the Irish Catholic found himself with no organic social institutions to which to relate himself. Instead, he relates himself to different authorities, who often pull him in opposing directions. There are three of these authorities, the new landlord, the priest, and the old aristocracy, whether they survived as landholders, defied the confiscation and became 'tories', or acquiesced in it and settled down in a diminished but still respected state. Cultural elements from the past continued to exercise their influence, especially that represented by the Irish language, while the Old English traditions seem to have kept their vitality to a considerable degree, especially in the towns. It is fortunate, then, that most of the surviving and available sources for the religious history of the Irish Catholics in the Restoration period fall into two groups. The first concerns the dioceses of Ferns, Ossory, and Waterford and Lismore, where the dominant culture was Old English. The second derives from the work of Oliver Plunkett, and is centred on Old Irish Ulster, with the substantial addition of Old English Meath. The rest of Ireland is thinly covered in the printed sources. There is a particularly interesting report on Limerick in 1671, but it concentrates on the city and only confirms the pattern of religious observance in the towns better documented for the south-east.

About 1680 the English publisher Moses Pitt planned an *English Atlas* in eleven volumes. The project was not financially successful, and only five volumes appeared (Oxford, 1680–82). The collection of the Irish material was undertaken by William Molyneux. Material for approximately twenty counties ended up among the manuscripts of Trinity College.[18] Less than a third has been printed. There are two reports on Co. Wexford, compiled by two new English Protestant settlers, Solomon Richards and Robert Leigh. Leigh is not particularly interested in religious matters. Richards is, and though it is very clear that he is strongly prejudiced against 'popery' it seems beyond question that his prejudices are honest in that he reports facts as they are known to him. There is a third report, also printed, on the barony of Forth in the south-east. The author, who does not name himself, is certainly a Catholic, almost certainly a priest, and may well have been named Sinnott. Naturally he too has his prejudices: it is interesting to see how his mind sometimes seems to slip back to the days before Cromwell, when so little had as yet changed in Forth. However, he may be taken as presenting with very great accuracy an image of the inhabitants of the barony as they saw themselves after the Restoration (both Richards and Leigh are agreed that nearly all the former gentry were still there, but as tenants, not as proprietors).

After an opening description that makes it clear that this is his native place and that he loves it — 'the whole barony, at a distance viewed in time of harvest, represents a well-cultivated garden' — he moves on to its great religious shrine of Our Lady's Island, where the traditional pilgrimage still flourished, as appears even more clearly from the long detailed description by Solomon Richards. Richards's disdain for what he regards as superstition is clear, but his description of the religious exercises of the pilgrimage is certainly factual, though possibly incomplete — the circuit of the island, some pilgrims being careful to keep one foot in the water and the other dry, great sinners making the circuit on their knees in the water, 'persons of no mean degree' walking barefoot from Wexford, though it was accepted that 'if any lady, through indisposition, be loath to wet her feet, then are women allowed to do it for them, they being present and paying half-a-crown for a fee'. 'The chiefest or most meritorious time is between the two Lady Days of August 15 and September 8'. He concentrates on those practices which suggest superstition: regrettably, but understandably, he makes no mention of prayers which may have been required, mentioning only the circuit of the island and an offering afterwards in the chapel, after which the pilgrim goes away. This basically hostile witness makes no reference to 'dancing, carousing and drinking' mentioned regularly at this time in connection with Catholic pilgrimages by similar observers.

Richards's account makes more credible the picture of an 'old-fashioned' but sober religious observance drawn by the anonymous author we may call Father Sinnott. He goes on to speak of the eighteen churches and thirty-three chapels, 'ruinated . . . since and during the late usurper's government', and adds 'there were very many crosses in public roads, and crucifixes, in private houses and churches in the said barony kept, builded of stone, timber or metal, representing the dolorous passion of our Saviour Jesus Christ, which, wherever found, were totally defaced, broken or burned by Cromwellian soldiers' (surviving examples in Co. Meath may be dated to about 1600). The people keep patron-days very devoutly, by penance and the Eucharist, followed by a feast and entertainment, 'cheerfully, piously and civilly'. They are 'very precise and exact' in keeping the Church's fasts. At wakes and funerals there are no 'rude eiulations or clamours, but counterfeit presentment of seeming sorrow'. They are hardworking and industrious: there is 'hardly any vagrant native beggar'. Even before Cromwell, though there was scarcely a native Protestant, the ministers of the Established Church lived peaceably among them and received their tithes and offerings.

One senses the same kind of society in the documentation for Bishop Luke Wadding, in particular his 'Notebook' and his letter of 4 May 1683 to the secretary of Propaganda describing his experiences during the Popish Plot.[19] He had been named coadjutor to the exiled Bishop Nicholas French in 1671, but had refused to be consecrated bishop, feeling he could work more effectively as a priest, first in New Ross and then in Wexford. He was arrested and brought to trial at the end of 1678, but he was able to plead in all honesty that he was not a bishop, nor a vicar general (Bishop French had died at Ghent the preceding August). It would appear that the opportunity to acquit him was gladly seized, for he had many Protestant friends, both lay and clerical, and the upshot of his trial was that he received formal permission to function in the chapel he had begun to build inside the walls of Wexford in 1674.

His fascinating 'Notebook' opens a window into his own life and Catholic life in Wexford town and its surroundings. It is clear that some Catholics in the town are propertied – Robert Leigh has noted that the merchants of New Ross are Catholic, and Solomon Richards that almost all the old proprietors of the barony of Forth are still on their ancestral lands, though now as tenants. The bishop's ancestral home was Ballycogley Castle, in Forth. His notebook refers to a 'cousin John Wadding' as being again at Ballycogley, no doubt as a tenant. In a list of family heirlooms the bishop still treasures, he notes ' a small glass bottle of blood which hath been in the castle of Ballycogley since my predecessors first came, what blood it is I know no more than that it was esteemed to be a drop of our Saviour's blood, brought by one

Luke Wadding's notebook, MS J5, p. 23, courtesy of the Franciscan Library, Killiney, Co. Dublin. Photograph by Donal Moore.

Gilbert Wadding who was at the taking of Jerusalem by Godfrey duke of Lorraine'.

This pride of the Norman centuries lived on in a man very much alive in his own century. At some stage he had his nephew Walter Wadding list the books in his library – over seven hundred in all, the solid foundation being the theological standbys of the Counter-reformation. The books reflecting a more personal choice are, in the area of spirituality, the classics of the French Jesuit and Salesian schools, with some that clearly reflect a very personal preference, Pierre de Camus for instance, 'the Walter Scott of Christian humanism' as Henri Brémond called him, and in the field of literature quite a number of the Jacobean dramatists and of the metaphysical poets. The bishop's own *Small Garland of Pious and Godly Songs,* published at Ghent in 1684, echoes the English metaphysicals, Crashaw in particular, a little faintly at times it may be, and also links with the two 'old script carol books' mentioned as being in his library, they in turn linking the carol singing that still survives in south Wexford to its medieval origins.

Of equal interest are his lists of catechisms, manuals and objects of devotion that he bought in quantity to pass on to others – beads and medals by the gross, some brought from France but more bought locally, in Wexford and New Ross: manuals and catechisms by the

---

Bookes

Bookes given and bestowed on Relations, freinds, benefactors, poore Gentry and widdowes, children etc. from the yeere 1668 I came to Ireland till the 1687 which I hope some did good.

I brought from Paris six dozen of christian diurnals composed by fr Causin the author of the holy court translated into English which I distributed as above	03	08	00
I brought 18 of introductions to a devout life composed by St Frances of Sale	01	16	00
I had one hundred dozen of Christian doctrine composed by fr P. Ledesma of which the pastors tooke part and I from time to time gave the rest the value at least of	02	10	00
I distributed at least twentie dozen of the smal catechisme of Bellarmine besids as much given by F. Rooth	01	03	00
Smal rituals for administringe sacraments brought 18 from Paris sent for 12 bought 6 Dublin	02	04	00
I had from Franke Rooth from Roterdam eighteen dozen of manuels printed in Gant in a smal volume of devout and godlie prayers Anno 1682 of which ten pounds was of my predecessor legacies six pounds fourteen shillings from my self besids twoe dozen given by Franke Rooth in all	18	00	00

(Ed. Patrick J. Corish in *Archiv. Hib., xxix* (1970), pp 88–9).

dozen – six dozen of *The Christian Diurnal* by the French Jesuit, Nicholas Caussin, eighteen dozen of *The Devout Life* by St Francis de Sales, a hundred dozen of the *Christian Doctrine* of Ledesma, forty dozen of Bellarmine's *Small Catechism,* perhaps forty dozen of 'a small manual of godly prayers and Don Antonio king of Portugal all in one little book', twelve dozen of the *Douai Catechism,* 'at least ten dozen' of his own *Small Garland of Pious and Godly Songs.* The good relationship with Protestants which stood him in good stead during the Popish Plot appears also in his 'Notebook'. The Catholic and Protestant parish registers indicate that the ministers of the Established Church were still requiring the wealthier Catholics to pay their dues as a condition of being allowed to marry in their own church, but this seems to have caused little if any friction. 'Mrs Shapoland, Ellen Bond' was a close personal friend, as passing entries in the notebook make clear: 'A holy court from London for Mrs Shapoland' (*The Holy Court* – the very title proclaims the baroque – was another highly popular work by Nicholas Caussin). He directed that she get his gardening tools after his death, knowing that she 'will give the use of them to the Catholic priest who will serve as pastor in Wexford', and also noted that 'the cithern belongeth to Mrs Ellen Shapoland'. Now Ellen Bond was a Catholic married to a Protestant (the Shaplands had settled in Co. Wexford in the reign of James I). They had been married by licence from the Protestant bishop, but their marriage is entered in the Catholic register, as are the baptisms of their children. Clearly Wexford town was finding its own way to cope with the problems of life.

The long detailed will of Bishop Phelan of Ossory,[20] drawn up in 1693, suggests that life in Kilkenny was in many ways like life in Wexford. It has already been noted that numbers of Catholic Butlers were restored to their lands thanks to the patronage of the duke of Ormond. It seems clear that a number of town Catholics in Kilkenny are in fairly comfortable circumstances, including some who had fled before Cromwell in 1650. The bishop has legacies for 'the duke's hospital' and 'Sir Richard Shee's hospital'. Naturally, the detail of Luke Wadding's 'Notebook' cannot be equalled in four pages, but there is quite enough to suggest great similarities between Catholic society in Kilkenny and Wexford.

There had been about fourteen priests in Ossory at the Restoration. When Bishop Phelan was appointed in 1669 he found thirty-four, but apparently some were not diocesans and drifted away. In 1678 there were twenty-eight diocesans and twenty-eight regulars. Twenty-three of the diocesans had been educated abroad. Because of the great number of regulars the clergy as a whole were badly distributed, too many in Kilkenny city, thin on the ground in some rural areas. Bishop Brenan of Waterford, who was having great trouble in setting up Catholic schools in his diocese, looked with envy at the number of schools in Ossory, again concentrated in Kilkenny. The indications then are of a considerable contrast between the urban and rural areas in the diocese. This impression is confirmed by the surviving diocesan regulations, for 1672 and 1676. Despite the fact that nearly all his diocesan clergy had some continental education the bishop did not pitch his hopes too high. All his priests were to be equipped with the catechism and with a text-book of moral theology ('cases of conscience'), but there is no mention of dogmatic theology ('controversies'). In country parishes, the parish priest may not be able to preach: if not, he is to get the services of a preacher every three months at least. The detailed spelling-out of set prayers to be recited at Mass – the Lord's Prayer, the Ave Maria, the Creed, the precepts of God and of the Church, the litanies – may indicate that a number of country priests were unable to preach. It may equally well indicate the bishop's conviction that regular repetition of the fundamentals was the most useful thing that could be done in the countryside. It fairly certainly indicates the increasing influence of the French *prône,* which contained such prayers as well as prepared sermons. It is interesting to see Bishop Phelan ordering the recitation of the psalm *De profundis* at Mass (so did Bishop Brenan of Waterford). This has traditionally been regarded as a specifically Irish practice, introduced, it has been claimed, in place of the Masses for the dead that ceased at the Reformation. It would be interesting to find out if it was a regular feature of the French *prône* of the time.

Bishop Phelan's regulations about the Eucharist give some indication that the fears expressed about Jansenism were not altogether without foundation. He is clearly no believer in frequent communion, and he has an over-spiritualised idea of how the Christian should approach the Eucharist that does seem to derive from Jansenism. He had been exiled to France as a young priest in the 1650s, and it was while he was in France over the next decade and more that his real theological education had taken place. His neighbour Luke Wadding in Wexford had also studied theology deeply in France at this time, but had attached himself to the Jesuit and Salesian schools. And if few people in Ossory were frequent communicants it may be taken as highly likely that this was not because they were Jansenists. The reason is rather to be sought in such things as a diocesan regulation of 1676 ordering sheelanagigs to be burned. Bishop Brenan in Waterford was ordering exactly the same thing that same year. A religion older than Trent was still strong in the countryside.

Bishop Brenan's diocese took in Waterford city and county and a considerable stretch of country in south Tipperary.[21] In south Tipperary some Butler landlords had been restored, notably Ormond's brother at Kilcash. Elsewhere many former Catholic landowners established themselves as leasehold tenants. Bishop Brenan has praise for some Protestant landowners for their kindness to Catholic priests even in time of persecution and for their willingness to give sites for Catholic chapels, but there are places where there is no chapel precisely because the landlord will not give a site. His clergy told him that the ministers of the Established Church were very polite so long as they received their fees for baptisms, marriages and funerals. He himself had been invited to call on the Protestant bishop and had done so. 'He showed me great politeness', Brenan reported, 'and manifested the best intentions not to cause me any molestation'. There was in fact little molestation from any quarter in the sense that the Catholics were free to carry out their religious functions. And yet here more than elsewhere, and in Waterford city particularly, one gets the distinct impression that while Catholics were free to be Catholics they were expected to take the consequences. Waterford corporation was completely unyielding in its exclusion of Catholic freemen. On Sundays while the Protestants were at church the Catholics were 'not allowed to hold any assembly, nor to walk through the city'. It was extremely dangerous to open a Catholic school, in contrast with the neighbouring diocese of Ossory. Bishop Brenan was very concerned at the problem of Catholic youth attending Protestant schools, and yet one senses that with the authorities the simple desire to prevent Catholic schools was stronger than any wish to proselytise.

The pattern of the clergy was very like that of neighbouring Ossory. In 1675 Brenan had thirty diocesan priests, with twenty religious. This comparative strength of the religious indicates that he too had a problem of distribution, the towns being favoured at the expense of the country districts (in 1687 Waterford city had three diocesan priests, five Franciscans, five Dominicans and five Jesuits, for a Catholic population probably not greatly exceeding 3,000). In the country parishes it could not be assumed that the priest was able to preach, but he was bound to catechise every Sunday and secure the services of a competent preacher at least once every three months. Other problems noted indicate slow progress, perhaps even some regression as the established patterns of society shifted and settled. Funerals and especially wakes are still not

Christian – 'ruin of souls, offence to God's majesty'. The regular and secular clergy are still contending over who has the right to conduct the funeral, and are in consequence inclined to give the laity what they want. The traditional patron-days or 'patterns' seem if anything to be becoming less Christian: feasting and drinking, without Mass or prayers, though apparently priests at times neglect Masses of precept in their own parishes to attend a 'pattern' in a neighbouring one.

Nevertheless Bishop Brenan was reasonably optimistic: 'the people, generally speaking, are very religious and pious, leading a Christian life without great faults or many scandals. They are most devoted to the Catholic faith and have great reverence for the apostolic see, and I hope, through the divine mercy, that in the future they may be able to receive more instruction so as to make more progress in Christian virtue'. His pattern for the priesthood from whom instruction must come appears in the *Schema vitae pastoralis* appended to his brief instructions of 1677. It is full of the sober gravity of the tridentine ideal. The priest is to be formed by a life of regular reception of the sacraments, prayer, recollection, mortification and study. This will fit him to be an effective preacher, again grave and sober, essaying no heights of eloquence, and on the other hand not pandering to his uninstructed hearers with stories of miracles and indulgences, or even by purveying straight gossip, but slowly raising them by instruction in the essential things, the virtues and vices, the daily prayers, the precepts of God and of the Church, the duties of men's state in life, the most prevalent and common sins. Unexciting perhaps, but not unattractive, and John Brenan, himself an attractive figure, clearly believed it could be achieved as he surveyed his diocese in 1677.

The northern ecclesiastical province appears in a clear light principally because of the correspondence of St Oliver Plunkett.[22] This province fell into two sharply contrasted sections. One was the primate's homeland, what had traditionally been the heart of the Pale: the county of Meath, the county of Westmeath shading into Irishry at its western edge, the county of Louth and the town of Drogheda. Here conditions were good. For a variety of reasons quite a number of Catholics had been restored to their estates, though many former landed proprietors, the archbishop's brother among them, were now tenants. However, the economic status of Catholics in general was sufficiently high to permit a considerable ease in general relations with Protestants. Archbishop Plunkett had many good friends among the Protestant laity and clergy. In consequence he was able to conduct a remarkable if unfortunately short-lived experiment in Jesuit-directed schools at Drogheda, with the tacit consent of the lords lieutenant, Berkeley and Essex. Protestants and Catholics attended these schools, as well as the young clergy who had been ordained in some numbers in the 1660s without any theological education. The schools opened in July 1670, but were forced to close in November 1673.

The diocese of Meath came through the decade of the interregnum without serious losses among its clergy. The fact seems clear, whatever the explanation: in 1660 Meath had about sixty priests, a situation without a real parallel. It may have been in the mind of Oliver Plunkett when in 1673 he complained that there were too many clergy, and in particular there were too many who were too independent of the bishop because too dependent on the gentry. One might gather that this was also the verdict of Bishop Cusack of Meath (1679–88). His diocesan statutes of 1686[23] declare that the clergy in general are so poorly educated that they must all seek approval from the bishop every year. The restrictions he imposed on the regular clergy were so severe as to draw down detailed reproach over fifty years later in the *De synodo diocesana* of Benedict XIV, himself no particular admirer of the religious life as it was then lived. These restrictions are so savage that one might very reasonably suspect they might have a Jansenist inspiration, but Bishop Cusack was educated in Rome, where he had been a fellow-student of Archbishop Oliver Plunkett. Making all allowance for the reserve with which these draconian decrees must be treated, it does seem as if at least the detritus of the friars were peddling a highly superstitious religion. Sir Henry Piers, writing of Westmeath in 1682, provides confirmation of the survival of old usages. He has already been cited as witness to the continuing cult of 'the holy hermit of Fore': elsewhere he speaks of what happens at pilgrimages, patterns, and wakes, the lewd obscene dancing, excessive drinking, broken heads and drunken quarrels, the keening – or, as he puts it, howling – mourners accompanying the funeral, pausing regularly at the ritual heaps of stones on the way to say a prayer and 'raise the howl' again. In many respects Westmeath was still an old land.

To cross from the lands of the old Pale into Gaelic Ulster is to step into a much older land. Here only two or three Catholic magnates had retained their estates, and the only one who counted, the earl of Antrim, was deeply bogged in debt. Yet a number of one-time landowners were now reasonably prosperous tenant-farmers, and despite their reduced fortune and status were still given the traditional deference by their former dependants. The same respect was extended to the 'tories', those who had refused to come to terms with the new order and had gone 'on their keeping', and in most cases were soon reduced by necessity to living by robbery.

The clergy of Gaelic Ulster had been least affected by the influence of the 'tridentine' seminary, and the case of Terence O'Kelly is an example of how little a stay in a seminary might affect a man's life-style. Archbishop O'Reilly had reported in 1660 that as far as numbers went they had not come too badly out of the previous decade: they had certainly done much better than in Leinster. Yet by the time Archbishop Plunkett arrived ten years later it is clear that there are serious problems – problems with celibacy, problems with drunkenness, problems arising from the fact that only a small number have a formal theological formation, and are not merely unable to preach but unable to give basic catechesis. One might perhaps venture a tentative opinion that standards were lower among the friars than among the diocesan clergy, if only because the friars were more deeply rooted in the old world that lay behind these problems, partly in itself no doubt, but even more in its decay. Certainly the picture of two friars prominent in bringing Archbishop Oliver Plunkett to Tyburn is not an attractive one – John McMoyer and Hugh Duffy in their 'friary' near Forkhill, deeply involved with the tories, a little muzzy for much of the time, always disposed to appeal to secular authority against an awkward bishop (needless to say, clergy of this kind were not all friars).

The religious practices of the laity may be expected to be deeply traditional, and in so far as they can be recovered they prove to be so (as already noted, it appears that some priests were unable to give even a basic catechesis). The problems around are still the old ones – a traditional society, quarrelsome, superstitious, its quarrels and superstitions tending to surface particularly in its most deeply-rooted religious observances, patterns, pilgrimages, wakes and funerals. Marriage practices do seem to be approaching much closer to the Christian norms, mainly perhaps because of the decline of the aristocracy, for surely only an aristocratic life-style could have sustained the traditional marriage customs. That gross sexual habits persisted is evidenced, for example, by the sharp tone of the legislation in the provincial synod of 1670 or the Kilmore diocesan synod of 1687,[24] excluding from all sacraments, unless there is established proof of repentance, those whom the Kilmore synod calls *gierador* – they might perhaps be described as 'living sheelanagigs': *mulierculae ... quae profitentur artem medendae impotentiae cum turpi ac prorsus detestabili in se experimento virilis potentiae.*

It is not so easy to bring into any kind of clear focus that 'permanent substratum of society', as Dr MacLysaght has called it, the great majority of the population, largely Gaelic even in the former Pale, outside the towns and exceptional districts such as Forth and Fingal. Even in the synodal legislation, it is reasonable to suspect, what surfaces reflects in the first instance the way of life of a former privileged class now in decline. This class naturally prefers to lament the past rather than try to come to terms with the present. This is true even of the older generation of those who had appeared as a truly revolutionary force in Ireland at the beginning of the seventeenth century, the Old English Catholic clergy. A number of them are permanently exiled, too compromised by their part in the politics of the 1640s to have any hope of return. From St Malo, John Lynch of Galway expressed his horror at the 'insolence' of the rising tenant farmers in the elegant Renaissance Latin he had learned in his father's school. Bishop Nicholas French of Ferns portrayed Ormond as the betrayer of Ireland in *The Unkinde Desertor,* published in 1676, two years before he died at Ghent: 'often have I lamented all alone for my dear country's desolation, and found my grief inconsolable, because I saw no end to their sufferings'.[25] What Ormond has betrayed is his Old English kin: the bishop's eyes are fixed on the 'English Wexford' he had known before Cromwell; he is out of touch with the fact that at the time he wrote the Catholics there were coming to terms with their change of fortune.

The Gaelic poets above all others are preoccupied with this theme of *fuit Ilium.* Their privileged class is facing extinction: there is no one to buy a poem: they are like hounds fighting over an empty dish. Even those remarkable compositions that ended up as folk-song are altogether aristocratic—'Eibhlín a Rún', 'Cill Chais', 'Éamonn a' Chnoic' and 'Seán Ó Duibhir a' Ghleanna'. Seán Ó Duibhir the huntsman was not really concerned with the woman glumly counting what geese the fox had left her but rather with the curtailment of his hunting pleasures, and saw no remedy except exile. There is Dáibhíd Ó Bruadair, by any standard a great poet, marrying the culture of the past with the new accentual metres. He is an embittered man, growing more bitter as times get harder, contempt in good taste his only weapon against louts and boors, dying in poverty in 1698, 'tramping the roads on foot ... reduced to old shoes'. Aodhagán Ó Rathaile (1670–1728) died bitterly dependent on 'Valentín Brún', an upstart and no very generous patron, 'composing songs for Master Thomas Browne and the rest of his lordship's children' at so much a song, because he had nothing else to live on. His secret thoughts were in his last song:

Rachad-sa a haithle searc na laoch don chill,
Na flatha fá raibh mo shean roimh éag do Chríost.

These were not the Brownes but the MacCarthys. No doubt it consoles
his ghost that he is buried among their tombs at Muckross.[26]

Observers from 'the Protestant interest' are hardly impartial
witnesses, but there is no doubt that they are noticeably better informed
at the end of the seventeenth century than at its beginning. Some we
have met already, Solomon Richards, Robert Leigh, Henry Piers and
others who wrote regional descriptions for the Molyneux Survey. Then
there are travellers like Thomas Dineley or John Dunton,[27] or William
Petty, the outstanding representative of the 'new philosophy' priding
itself on exact observation. They are useful in that they see things from
another angle, useful too in that they sometimes note down things that
Catholics would not think of noting because they take them so much for
granted. Dineley, for instance, seems to be the first witness to the
established tradition of St Patrick's Day, when 'the Irish of all stations
and conditions wear crosses in their hats ... and the vulgar
superstitiously wear shamrocks ... very few of the zealous are found
sober at night'. He and others note the tendency of ostensibly religious
occasions, such as patterns and pilgrimages, to end in a drunken riot, or
indeed for drunken riots to develop without any clear reason at all. They
note the superstitious atmosphere at wakes and funerals. Dineley notes
that in the cities and towns they bury 'without any unusual ceremony'
(it might be remembered that in 1635 Sir William Brereton had noted
keening even in Dublin). Dunton, who can hardly be described as
squeamish or over-sensitive, seems genuinely shaken by some aspects of
the 'wake-games'. To show how blind and irrational the Irish papist
religion is (here he need not be assumed to be impartial) he gives an
account of 'passive' assistance at Mass (which he asserts is based on
observation): 'while the Pater is repeating from their altar, you shall
hear others thumping their breasts and muttering an Ave Maria, the
Credo, or Mea culpa, as my own senses assure me'. Petty likewise is
both patronising and exact:[28]

> there is much superstition among them, but formerly much more than is
> now; for as much as by the conversation of Protestants, they became
> ashamed of their ridiculous practices, which are not *de fide*. As for the
> richer and better-educated sort of them, they are such Catholics as are in
> other places. The poor, in adhering to their religion, which is rather a
> custom than a dogma amongst them, they seem rather to obey their
> grandees, old landlords, and the heads of their septs and clans, than God.

Elsewhere Petty plays with the thought that an increasing prosperity would reconcile the Protestants and 'the richer and better educated sort' of Catholics. In Restoration Ireland it was perhaps not altogether an unreasoned hope. There are indications that some Catholics shared it, but it did not survive the treaty of Limerick.

James II had little except religion in common with his Irish subjects. He felt they should be content with prerogative toleration and a limited share of office, but they were determined to have a great deal more. These differences emerged clearly at the 'Patriot Parliament' of 1689. An Act for Liberty of Conscience guaranteed religious freedom, allowed the Church of Ireland to retain its property, but insisted that all were to pay tithe for the support of the clergy of their own denomination. Allowing for an element of expediency in its decision, the parliament (dominated by the Old English) produced legislation that was a landmark of religious toleration in an environment hostile to it. They reasserted the political claim, now the common property of Catholic and Protestant, of the kingdom of Ireland ruled by its king, lords, and commons, but they stopped very far short of the 'establishment' of the Catholic Church that Rinuccini had in effect demanded forty years before. The laws passed by the 1689 parliament would have restored the Old English Catholics to the 'political nation' on terms they regarded as acceptable. The loss of the war left them no assurance except the treaty of Limerick.

William of Orange had enough of other troubles on his hands to have a real interest in a speedy ending to the war in Ireland, so the Catholics had some bargaining power. The article dealing with religion was, however, ambiguous. It promised the Catholics such freedom of worship as was consistent with the laws of Ireland and such as they had enjoyed under Charles II. This was riddled with ambiguities. William's further undertaking to recommend parliament to give even greater security piled ambiguity on ambiguity. No Catholic had sat in the Irish House of Commons since the Restoration, and Catholics had little to expect from 'the Protestant interest'. In fact, the treaty of Limerick was distinctly less favourable than the Ormond peace of 1649. The undertakings then given had not been honoured, and now after another lost war Catholics would soon be definitively excluded from 'the political nation'. Once again the problems of being a Catholic in Ireland will present themselves in a new context.

4 'Worsted in the Game'

The 'new context' for the Catholics of Ireland was the 'Penal Code', that body of laws enacted in the main in the first quarter of the eighteenth century. Their cumulative effect was summed up in 1759 by John Bowes, chief baron of the exchequer, when he declared that the law did not presume an Irish Catholic to exist except for the purposes of punishment. Exclusion from the political nation began when the Irish parliament, against the wishes of William of Orange, refused to ratify the treaty of Limerick. William was himself a Calvinist, and accustomed to the relatively tolerant atmosphere of the United Provinces, though even here Catholics did not participate in the political system. He was also dependent on Catholic powers while the war against France lasted, though this pressure lessened when it ended with the peace of Ryswick (1697). The international situation turned further against Catholic interests during the War of Spanish Succession (1701–13). Inevitably, the English succession was very much an issue in this new coalition of the European powers against Louis XIV. Anne, the last of the Stuarts in the direct Protestant line, was queen of England from 1702 to 1714. She was personally a committed Anglican, and during her reign the penal code was in substance enacted. Further legislation was passed over the years while the Protestant succession was still considered insecure. A long peace with France, lasting until the 1740s, helped to consolidate the Hanoverians, and from about 1730 the Catholic Church in Ireland enjoyed a reasonable measure of toleration, not seriously disrupted by the war scares of the next decade.

There is a wide measure of agreement on the nature and purpose of the penal code directed against the Irish Catholics, so a summary of its main provisions will suffice. In the words of W. E. H. Lecky, it was designed 'to make them poor and to keep them poor ... to degrade them into a servile caste'. Those provisions that were taken seriously were directed against Catholic property, not against the practice of the Catholic religion. Above all, they were directed against Catholic landed property, for land was the basis of political power. Here the penal code was meant to bite and made to bite, to reach what Edmund Burke was to call its 'vicious perfection'. There was a very real fear that in some way or another Catholics might recover their estates: the addresses at the opening of parliament in the early years of the century continue to stress the dangers of popery and 'the fatal consequences of reversing the outlawries of persons attainted of high treason for the rebellion in 1641 and 1688'. The Catholic share of Irish land had fallen from 59 per cent in 1641 to 22 per cent in 1688, and to 14 per cent in 1703 after fresh attainders. By the 1770s it had fallen to 5 per cent as a result of the penal code. Existing Catholic estates were to be split up by insisting that inheritance be by gavelkind, not by primogeniture, and by various enactments rewarding sons who conformed to the Established Church during their father's lifetime. Legislation in 1709 ruled out any possibility that Catholics might acquire land illegally. It did this by introducing the 'Protestant discoverer', who, if he could prove in court that property had been illegally acquired, received that property as his reward. This provision made the laws against Catholic acquisition of property self-enforcing.

Catholics were effectively excluded from the professions and public life by a series of legal enactments. No explicit legislation seems to have been required to exclude them from town corporations: this was achieved by the very structures of society. Yet it was precisely in the towns that Catholics were able to accumulate wealth, even though it had been the policy of the Commonwealth regime in the 1650s to exclude propertied Catholics from the towns altogether, and this had been confirmed by legislation in 1667 and again in 1704. Successive enactments severely hindered Catholics who wished to set up in manufacture. On the other hand, no concerted effort was made to exclude them from trade, especially the provisions trade, and it was here that Catholic wealth grew, even in Dublin, and by the end of the century, perhaps especially in Dublin.

There were many enactments regulating marriages between Protestants and Catholics, and new legislation under this head continued well after legislation in general had slackened off. Penalties against Catholic priests officiating at such marriages were stepped up. In 1725 they were to be adjudged guilty of felony, and a few were actually put to death. As late as 1745 such marriages conducted by a Catholic priest were declared null in law. Overall, however, it is clear that this marriage legislation was motivated by a concern for property and not by strictly religious intolerance. It was designed to ensure that if these marriages did take place any property settlement would be in favour of the Protestant interest.

Because the primary concern of the penal code was with property, there were large and never resolved ambiguities when it came to deal with religious practice. The dilemma of the Established Church after 1660 has already been noted. On the one hand, its claim to be the 'establishment' implied a duty to provide a 'Christian presence' in the country at large, in contrast with the sects, who provided for particular interests and who might or might not be tolerated as the political climate might dictate, and as the century advanced 'a toleration to all dissenters whose errors or superstitions affect themselves alone' became more and more acceptable. On the other hand, any attempt to give effect to this claim to 'establishment' by mounting a serious mission to the country as a whole would raise very awkward problems because of the large-scale confiscations, even if the resources of the Church would have allowed for such a mission. In fact they never did. The problem was particularly acute in the years after the revolution of 1688. Politically, many churchmen found the revolution distasteful. It might be noted that seven bishops in the House of Lords protested against the first breach of the treaty of Limerick in 1697, and there is evidence of disquiet about civil laws regulating popish priests in marriage matters, because marriage as a sacrament was a concern of the Church and the priests, despite their popery, were validly-ordained Christian ministers.

It might perhaps have been more logical to have rested content with laws designed to ensure that Catholics could never again become a political or economic threat to the settlement, and to have allowed them to practise their religion within this framework. This in fact is fairly close to what actually happened, though, because since laws against religious practice were introduced and did not prove enforceable, the civil authorities were not in a position to oversee or in any way control the development of the Catholic mission. In any case, no such clear division between political power and religious practice was accepted at the beginning of the century. What was sometimes referred to as 'popery in the gross' was not seen simply as a religion, but rather as a dangerous and untrustworthy political system, biding its time for another attempt to overthrow the settlement by force.

An Act of 1697 was entitled 'An Act for banishing all papists exercising any ecclesiastical jurisdiction and all regulars of the popish clergy out of the kingdom.' They were to be gone by 1 May 1698, and most of them went. This distinction in favour of the diocesan clergy had already appeared in the 1670s, but the renewed attempt to banish all church authority, had it been consistently enforced, would have reduced the Catholic Church in Ireland to the status of a very precarious mission. As the Emperor Leopold, lately William's Catholic ally, noted, it aimed at 'the entire extirpation of the Catholic religion'. The next major legislation, the Registration Act of 1704, might seem to confirm that this was indeed the overall design, even if it was to be carried out by degrees, possibly to avoid offence to the Catholic powers. Every popish priest in Ireland was required to register in court, giving name, address, age, parish, date and place of ordination and name of ordaining prelate, and furnishing two securities of £50 each that he would be of good behaviour and not leave the county for which he was registered. In all, 1089 priests registered, and in consequence were free to perform their functions. The legislation, however, was quite explicit that no new registrations would be accepted. In consequence, within a generation at most there would be no Catholic priests left.

This design collapsed in a few years. Following the invasion scare of 1708, it was decided to require of all registered priests the oath of abjuration of the Stuarts first imposed on government officials in 1701 when, on the death of James II, Louis XIV had recognised his son as James III. The treaty of Limerick had required of Catholics a straightforward oath of allegiance, 'and no other'. However, many Protestants who might have felt unhappy with this provision as being insufficient would have had difficulties in taking the oath now proposed. It demanded that a person swear that he believed in conscience that the exiled Stuarts had no title to the throne; that he would support 'to the utmost of his power' the Protestant succession; and that in all this he was acting 'heartily, willingly and truly'. If the oath posed difficulties for a Protestant, it posed greater difficulties for a Catholic, and insuperable difficulties for a Catholic priest. Only thirty-three priests are known to have taken it, and the total cannot have been significantly greater. There is evidence of some Protestant sympathy for their refusal, and the administration was left wondering what to do.

By refusing to take the oath the priest lost the benefits of registration. Any attempt to discharge his functions exposed him to banishment. Magistrates were empowered to summon any papist over the age of sixteen and require him, under oath, to reveal when and where he had heard Mass, who celebrated the Mass, and who were present, as well as to give information on the whereabouts of 'any popish regular clergyman, who may be disguised, concealed, or itinerant in the county'. The pattern of enforcement varied, ranging from active and sustained persecution to sympathetic connivance. Here too professional 'discoverers' made their appearance, hoping by securing a conviction to obtain the substantial reward the law offered. They did not meet with the same success as the 'discoverers' of illegal property. Catholic religious practice was seriously disrupted for some years, but many Protestants, even in Dublin, detested this new type of 'discoverer', or, as he soon came to be known, the 'priest-catcher', as much as did Catholics. On 27 November 1718 one of the most notorious, John Garzia, presented Anthony Brien, who had registered as parish priest of Rathfarnham but had not taken the oath of abjuration. Some of the Protestant jury were unwilling to convict, and did so only after being recalled for a further charge from the bench. It was noted that 'a great many English and Irish are sorry for the said Brien, knowing him to be a very good honest man, who maintained a poor helpless charge'.[1] In 1722 John Molloy complained to the House of Commons 'that one Samuel Dye a reputed Protestant ... called this deponent a priest-catcher, a rogue, with many ignominious names, collaring this deponent and most grossly treating him where there were many Romans, either to curry favour with them or to raise a mob about him as this deponent verily believes by the often repetitions he made of the name of priest-catcher'.[2] Molloy had reason to fear. Some years before, 'some hundreds of the popish inhabitants of this city [Dublin] in a riotous and tumultuous manner assembled in Fishamble Street and in other parts of the town, in order to waylay and insult one Henry Oxenard ... crying out a priest-catcher, and thereupon threw stones, brickbats and dirt at him in so violent a manner that his life was greatly endangered ...'[3] He escaped, but the constables sent to protect him were barely sufficient and several of them were wounded. Even in Dublin the priest-catcher's reward was poor enough return for the risks he ran.

What might be described as active if sporadic persecution of the Catholic clergy continued until about 1730. One might well ask if it may have been during these twenty years or so that the priest began to emerge as a kind of folk-hero, enjoying wide support among a defeated people for his successful resistance to unjust laws. The harrying was not consistent enough to prevent the re-establishment of the Catholic mission. Even had the will been there, the administration simply lacked the resources. The police-force was rudimentary. Communications were very bad. The mob posed a threat in Dublin itself, and further down the country it was a very great deterrent to an over-zealous magistrate. In any case, the will was not there. General control of the law-enforcing apparatus was in the hands of the Irish administration, responsible not to the Dublin parliament but to the English executive. The English executive allowed the 'popery laws' to pass because 'divide and rule' was the cheapest way of controlling what it saw as its Irish colony. Enforcement, even had it been possible, would have been expensive, and in any case the Irish ascendancy was not consistently willing to face the problems enforcement would bring.

By about 1730, then, the Catholics were allowed to practise their religion if they paid the price. The price was high. Macaulay's rhetoric is not misplaced:[4]

> In Ireland there was peace. The domination of the colonists was absolute. The native population was tranquil with the ghastly tranquillity of exhaustion and despair. There were indeed outrages, robberies, fire-raisings, assassinations. But more than a century passed away without one general insurrection ... Nor was this submission the effect of content, but of mere stupefaction and brokenness of heart. The iron had entered into the soul. The memory of past defeats, the habit of daily enduring insult and oppression, had cowed the spirit of the unhappy nation. There were indeed Irish Roman Catholics of great ability, but they were to be found everywhere except in Ireland ... One exile became a marshal of France. Another became prime minister of Spain. If he had stayed in his native land he would have been regarded as an inferior by all the ignorant and worthless squireens who drank the glorious and immortal memory.

It may call for some nuance, but not much. The conquered people had to pay the full price of their defeat. Yet as part of the pattern of that defeat the laws against their clergy were not consistently enforced and the Church established by law did not lead any campaign of evangelisation. In these circumstances, the Catholics once again reorganised, not a mission, but a Church. As early as 1730 almost every diocese had its bishop, in some cases after a very long vacancy. For instance, Kilmore, vacant since 1669, received a bishop in 1728. These bishops had no legal standing at all, and especially in the earlier years led a rather furtive existence. Nevertheless, their very presence made organisation possible. The registration of 1704 provided the basis for the parish system, even though the registered priests functioned illegally after 1710, and their successors were never legal. Numbers of religious had registered as parish-priests in 1704, and even before this date there were complaints that they were returning from banishment: as a pamphleteer complained in 1703, they concealed themselves 'under the guise of physicians and other professions ... others being better known ... choose to abide imprisonment, where by the interest of their gaolers they easily obtain leave to teach as schoolmasters and have their daily Masses and thereby all desired opportunities of ordaining others'.[5] The religious orders survived their more rigorous proscription as easily as the seculars survived theirs. Their numbers soon increased rapidly, and they managed to establish communities and even novitiates.

There was never penal legislation against nuns, possibly because they were few in number and because there were none in Dublin during the years when the worst legislation was passed. Galway was their stronghold, and the first group came to Dublin in 1712, but until the foundation of native congregations at the end of the century the number of both houses and religious remained small and they led undisturbed lives, keeping boarding schools for girls: the Report on the State of Popery presented to the House of Lords in 1731 refers to the 'nunnery in Channel Row' that 'commonly goes under the name of a boarding school' as a fact simply to be noted without comment.

A school-system for the Catholic population in general was also established. Because the schoolmaster was a major cultural factor, the law tried to suppress him perhaps even more completely than the priest. As early as 1695 it was enacted that 'no person of the popish religion may publicly teach school or instruct youth; or in private houses teach or instruct youth except only the children . . . of such private family'. The gap was filled by the 'hedge-schools'. A legend that still needs much disentangling has gathered about them. That they came into existence quite early is proved by the frequent prosecutions of Catholic schoolmasters during the really bad years, though they often seem to have escaped by simply moving on. In due course the proscription of the schoolmaster broke down also. The Report of 1731 disclosed many Catholic schools – one in every parish, the bishop of Clonfert reported from Catholic Connacht. As might be expected, the situation was worst in Ulster. The reaction of the ascendancy was to set up the Charter schools in 1733, avowedly to make Protestants of the children of the poor. Overall, their effect was quite marginal, though at the time the Catholic Church authorities regarded them as a definite threat and in consequence set out to systematise Catholic schooling. By the second half of the century there was in effect a Catholic parish school system over much of the country.

What this general Catholic reorganisation achieved was by any standards creditable. That there should be shortcomings is only to be expected, given the handicaps under which it worked. With very few exceptions, the bishops were worthy men, 'who maintained a poor helpless charge'. In due course respectful obituary notices begin to appear in the papers, for example of Bishop Mulligan of Ardagh in 1739, 'this illustrious defunct . . . a religious man of the order of the Hermits of St Augustine . . . one of the most profound humility and unfeigned piety'.[6] The most serious charge brought against bishops deemed to be unworthy was that they were prepared to ordain all who offered a fee. Though only a few bishops are mentioned by name, it is nevertheless clear that ordination was too easily come by in early eighteenth-century Ireland, and that too many were ordained, possibly because ordination to the priesthood provided one of the few means of advancement that lay open. By about 1740 a number of bishops were expressing concern at the increased numbers of the clergy, many of them, it was alleged, unlettered and unable to find a parochial appointment. They were particularly concerned by the great increase in the numbers of the friars.

It was the threat seen in the Charter schools that prompted attempts to remedy the situation, but these efforts broadened into a review of the whole pastoral mission. What imperfect statistics emerged from the investigation would seem to indicate, firstly, that there were not enough parishes, the bigger parishes needing division or the appointment of an assistant, though registered parish priests were legally forbidden to have one; secondly, the overall number of clergy was not excessive, though some might be unsuitable and the overall distribution was not good; and thirdly, the friars had increased much more rapidly than the seculars, being almost equal to them in number, so that if the parish was to be the basic unit of pastoral care their numbers did pose a problem.

After carefully seeking information, Pope Benedict XIV issued a decree reorganising the Irish Church early in 1751. While the pope was not against the religious life as such, he did have serious reservations about the way it was actually being lived in his time. His decisions were heavily weighted against the Irish friars, in some respects subjecting them more strictly to episcopal control than the general discipline of the Church laid down (though it might be noted that Benedict took some steps to subject the religious orders more strictly to the bishops in the Church as a whole). Henceforth, all regular clergy in Ireland had to live in community; the bishop was given wide powers even over this community — specifically, he might transfer regular clergy within his diocese, but their superior might not transfer them without the bishop's consent; novices might not be received in Ireland, but only in the continental houses.

These decisions led to a rapid drop in the numbers of the friars and a marked restriction on their work among the people. Within twenty years their numbers had halved, and they continued to decline. This was a truly revolutionary development, ending the position the friars had enjoyed since the effective beginning of the Counter-reformation, and to some extent, especially in Gaelic Ireland, at least since the fifteenth century. From now on, they could not pose a serious alternative to the parish system of pastoral care. On the other hand, standards of education improved, among both regular and secular clergy. The friar had to make his novitiate in Catholic Europe, and the secular was not ordained unless he undertook to go to a continental college to study theology. The trouble was that numbers of them did not come back, and in the case of some who did there were indications that a course in theology did not necessarily produce a good parish priest. Finally, if the complaint earlier in the century had been that there were too many priests, before it ended one gets a distinct impression that there were possibly too few to meet within a parish system the needs of a growing population.[7]

5 The Shaping of a Religious Culture

The preceding chapter has sketched out in summary form the main provisions of the penal code and the main lines of organisation of the mission of the Catholic Church. This mission must now be explored in more detail, in an attempt to answer the more subtle question, what this mission effected, what was the quality of Christian life it produced. To begin with, it cannot be expected that this quality of life will be uniform. It has already been noted that almost from the beginning of the Counter-reformation mission there were differences as between one region and another, and as between the different social strata. These differences persisted: it is not historical to see the penal laws as having reduced all Catholics to the same general level of deprivation.

Connacht might be set apart from the other provinces because it still had a sizeable number of Catholic landowners, Ulster because it had scarcely any and because in much of it there was a sizeable Protestant population. Leinster and Munster may be taken together, again because they had been similarly affected by the plantations, though regional differences may be expected within this wide area. It has already been noted that the towns require separate treatment, and this becomes even more necessary in the eighteenth century as Catholic merchants amassed wealth by trade. Among the towns, Dublin might well be considered separately, not only because its Catholic history is comparatively well documented for the period, but also because, at least in the earlier part of the century, the conditions of existence there were in some respects exceptional.

Dublin, in its historic core, or what is left of it, looks different even today — a city of alien brick. As already noted, at the end of the Commonwealth it was three-quarters Protestant. However, it grew rapidly in size after the Restoration, and a teeming Catholic population, to a considerable extent Irish-speaking, developed in the 'liberties' of the old city. Exceptionally, the trade of Dublin had begun to pass to Protestants in the first half of the seventeenth century, but here too a prosperous Catholic merchant community developed in the first half of the eighteenth.[1]

Catholics had to keep a low profile in this city, which was the seat of government and parliament, and was relatively well policed. On the

82

other hand, its very size made it easier to live there undisturbed. In the early years of the century a number of Catholic bishops based themselves in Dublin because they were afraid to live permanently in their own dioceses. For the same reason Dublin became a refuge for many a clerical 'drop-out', who earned his living by assisting at clandestine marriages as a 'couple-beggar' or 'tack-'em' and spent a great deal of what he earned in the ale-houses of the city.

Nevertheless, even in Dublin the common pattern was soon established, that Catholics might practise their religion provided they kept their heads prudently low, and kept them particularly low while parliament was in session. It was only at times of particular tension that it was judged unsafe to use the Mass-houses. In the years after the Registration Act attempts were made to discourage Masses in private houses, and even in the bad years after 1709 it would appear that Sunday services in the Mass-houses were interrupted only intermittently. It is true that in these years the 'priest-catchers' were active in Dublin, but already they had found reason to fear the anger of the mob in the liberties. Archbishop Byrne had to go into hiding in 1712. The 'priest-catcher' John Garzia finally ran him to earth, effecting an arrest about 2 o'clock in the morning of Sunday 1 June 1718. Yet when the archbishop finally appeared in court on 13 November 1719 he was discharged because Garzia did not put in an appearance as prosecutor. It seems clear that the government had been seriously embarrassed by his arrest, and was unwilling to convict him to allow a man like Garzia to collect his reward.

While there was serious harassment of the clergy during these years, the government in fact was having the worst of both worlds, unwilling to try extermination as in the 1650s and at the same time losing the opportunities for control provided by the Registration Act. By 1730 a parish system was clearly in existence, together with a number of churches of friars. The 1731 Report on the State of Popery lists thirteen Mass-houses, four of them very recently built. They were unpretentious and hidden buildings: one of them is described as 'an old stable . . . at the back of the Lord of Ely's house in Hawkins St.' A detailed description, compiled not unsympathetically by a Protestant in 1749, indicates that by this date they have attained to some interior dignity, but Rocque's map of 1756 depicts them very graphically, built in back yards, expanding irregularly to fill the available space, entered through alleyways and not directly from the public street.[2]

Diocesan statutes for 1730 contrast strikingly with the reticent regulations hastily drawn up when Archbishop Byrne went into hiding

This section of Rocque's map shows (marked with a cross) the Catholic parish chapels of Dirty Lane and Cook St., the Augustinians in John's Lane and the Carmelites in Wormwood Gate. The Augustinian 'nunry' in Mullinahack is also marked.

in 1712.[3] A Catholic parish system of pastoral care was firmly established, though the clergy of the Established Church continued to assert their rights to fees for baptisms, marriages and funerals. In addition to the Sunday sermon or catechesis, in the city parishes the children were assembled every Saturday in the chapel for instruction, and householders and parish-priests were ordered to arrange for instruction each Sunday for the servants of the house. The parish priest was also ordered to have a schoolmaster in his parish for catechesis, and to oversee his work. A passing reference in the will of Archbishop Luke Fagan (d. 1733), 'I give to Mr Nary for the use of the charitable infirmary fifteen pounds',[4] suggests some system of social care of which little seems to be known.

From the second decade of the century the friars had had the devotion of exposition of the Blessed Sacrament on Sundays and holy days – prudentially, while parliament was not in session.[5] The diocesan clergy seem to have disapproved – partly perhaps from fear of government reaction, partly because they did not like this kind of devotion anyway (by mid-century there must have been little to fear from the government, for rosaries were on public sale in the main streets of the city, and it was claimed that even some Protestants carried them secretly in their pockets). The development of confraternities seems to have come more slowly, though here again the friars took the lead, drawing the laity into church devotions, in a way that did not altogether commend itself to Archbishop Lincoln, who complained in 1761 of processions of 'three or four lubberly fellows with scapulars about their shoulders, the same of the belt with wax tapers in their hands'.

'Never was a city better provided with learned and zealous instructors than Dublin is at present' a Jesuit wrote from the city in 1747, 'we now begin to have vespers sung and sermons preached in the afternoons. You see hereby how peaceable times we enjoy'. From 1761 there is an account of Sunday services at the Dominican chapel in Bridge St. – a sermon in Irish at the seven o'clock Mass, in English at ten, exposition of the Blessed Sacrament at eleven followed by benediction at noon, no doubt not altogether to the liking of the diocesan clergy, with vespers and the rosary in the afternoon, and another sermon. It is clear that the strictly religious restrictions of the penal laws are over. The consolidation of this position was the work of Archbishop Carpenter (1770–86). Himself a noted Irish scholar, he had commissioned an 'Irish form of preparation for Sunday Mass' that was in itself a wide-ranging exposition of Christian doctrine and must indeed have lengthened the ceremony considerably. His concern for education appears too from the fact that at his death there were forty-seven parish schools in Dublin, with 1,770 pupils. By now Catholic schools were legal, and advertisements for grammar schools began to appear in the newspapers, successors to earlier ventures, tolerated though illegal, like the 'seminary' established in Saul's Court by John Murphy and John Austin, S.J., who in his boyhood had been a protégé of Dean Swift.[6]

There are indications that even within the diocese of Dublin it was possible to make rather better provision for general catechesis in the city than in the country districts. It is nevertheless unlikely that the level of achievement was better than what was attained overall. The city poor may well have been the poorest of all. Violence and drunkenness were endemic. Writing in 1802 Archbishop Troy noted that these and related problems were worse in the city than in the country districts.

Here, however, may be the best place to consider certain developments that of their nature had most effect among the middle classes, especially in the towns, the growth of a reading Catholic public and a possibly related issue, the alleged growth of Jansenism among Irish Catholics in the eighteenth century. By the time of Archbishop Carpenter the Catholic merchants of Dublin were no longer living the ghetto-like existence they had prudently adopted earlier in the century, but had emerged with a new cultural and social confidence. True, habits of caution died hard: in a revealing note to the internuncio at Brussels in 1776 the archbishop asked him to address all correspondence 'to a private person as follows: To Dr Carpenter, Usher's Island, Dublin'. But even at the beginning of the century the growth of the Dublin book trade had made it clear that there was now a steady market for religious books. The eighteenth-century penal code had introduced no new legislation, but statutes of Edward VI and James I would have entailed total proscription had they been put into effect. That they were still remembered is clear, for example, from Bullingbrooke's *The duty and authority of the justices of the peace and parish officers for Ireland* (Dublin, 1766), but here as elsewhere duty and authority was one thing and what happened was another. From the very beginning of the century sporadic protests and seizures indicate that Catholic books were being printed in Ireland as well as being imported from the continent. Dr Cornelius Nary, the learned parish priest of St Michan's, began a lifetime of publication with *Prayers and Meditations* for the use of his parishioners in 1705.

The booksellers' lists[7] give some indication of what they read, bearing in mind, naturally, that a book may be regularly on the lists either because it is selling well or because it is scarcely selling at all, so that it is necessary to apply a control by taking some account of the number of Irish printings of any particular book. By these tests, certain established favourites emerge. There is the translation by Thomas Hawkins of *The Holy Court* by the French Jesuit, Nicholas Caussin, chaplain to Louis XIII; William Darrell, the English Jesuit, especially his *Moral Reflections on the Epistles and Gospels of every Sunday throughout the year;* Robert Manning's *Moral Entertainments* and controversial works; *The Poor Man's Catechism* by the Benedictine, John Anselm Mannock; *An Essay on the Rosary* by the Irish Dominican, John O'Connor; *The Christian Directory,* a lasting classic by the English Jesuit, Robert Parsons; and the *Introduction to the Devout Life* by St Francis de Sales, which was a great favourite. But the most popular spiritual writer, beyond all question, was Richard Challoner. His revision of the Rheims translation (the New Testament first appeared in 1749) remained the standard Catholic version until quite recent times, as did his translation of *The Imitation of Christ.* His own works, *The Garden of the Soul,* for example, *Think well on't* and *Meditations for every day of the year* were widely used.

It will be immediately evident that most of this reading is imported, but it should also be noted that it lies in a very definite tradition. If it has a single tap-root it is the French spirituality, Salesian and Jesuit, of the early seventeenth century – after the Bible, the spiritual master of Challoner was St Francis de Sales. This suggests we should be very careful in applying the world 'Jansenistic' to Irish Catholic spirituality, all the more so as it has been conclusively shown that the Irish institutions in France, particularly in Paris, where most of the diocesan clergy were educated, were quite positively anti-Jansenist in the eighteenth century.[8] It is true that at the beginning of the eighteenth century the papers of the Brussels nunciature are preoccupied with the problem of Jansenism in Ireland, but when, for example, we find the imprisoned archbishop of Dublin, on 8 July 1718, smuggling out of his prison at the nuncio's request a letter accepting the papal condemnation of Jansenism contained in the bull *Unigenitus,* signed by himself and his suffragans, and doubtless praying that it would in fact reach the nuncio, for if it were intercepted he himself would have provided all the evidence needed to convict him, it is hard to avoid the conclusion that the concern expressed by an over-anxious bureaucrat need not be taken too seriously, and, all in all, this would appear to be the case. Even if all the nuncio's concerns are taken seriously, they do not add up to much.

'Jansenism', then, can be dismissed as an explanation of the development of any stern or anxious strain in Irish Catholic morality, but that such a strain did develop can hardly be questioned. For the reading, middle-class, Catholics, its source, or at any rate its immediate source, should probably be sought in Richard Challoner. Francis de Sales was his master, but his experiences as a bishop in penal-day London induced in him a streak of sadness verging on severity quite foreign to St Francis. Charles Butler's remark is well known: 'He was very cheerful, and the cause of cheerfulness in others, but he stopped very short of mirth'. Not that the Irish Catholics had to turn to Challoner's writings to develop a sad severity: they too shared his experience of living under penal legislation. It is hard to be precise in this matter when dealing with the bulk of the population. It may be that with them this stern morality was a nineteenth-century development, but the more one considers this proposition the more reservations present themselves. The fact that they too had the experience of living under a repressive code cannot be lightly discounted. In so far as one can probe towards a strictly religious explanation, it may well be that the sense of personal relationship with God established, however imperfectly, by tridentine catechesis, remained in the shadow of an essentially pagan notion of God as an arbitrary being waiting to punish.

The quality of religious life in the other towns is in many ways like that of Dublin. Indeed in some respects they were more favourably placed, farther from the central authority, smaller and therefore more tightly-knit communities, with, especially in the earlier years of the century, a more solidly-established merchant class that, as has been seen, would appear to have persisted through all the vicissitudes of the seventeenth century, with an economic power that gave it social weight even though it had no voice in local politics. In Cork, for example, the centre of the growing provisions trade, the Catholic merchants appear as early as 1708 as a body quite capable of standing up to the Protestant city council, their wealth buttressed by the support of the whole Catholic community: as the pamphleteer who called himself Alexander the Coppersmith complained in 1737, 'if a papist at the gallows wanted an ounce of hemp, he'd skip the Protestant shops and run to Mallow Lane to get it'. These laymen of substance may be glimpsed in other towns – the merchants of Limerick prepared in 1708 to go further surety for priests at £100 each, or those in Clonmel in 1713, where they were known to attend Mass and shelter priests, encouraged perhaps because some Protestants connived at what they were doing. In these towns too the middle class Catholics became a reading people. Cork and Waterford had their own publishers, and as the years went by there were few towns without a bookseller, even if books were only part of his trade, like Tim Nowlan, 'bookseller and seedsman', of Tullow St., Carlow.

The towns too had more priests than the countryside. Numbers may not have been of first importance earlier in the century, though there is some reason to believe that even when it was a general complaint that there were too many priests there were not enough effective workers in the country parishes. For example, only fourteen priests were returned for Co. Louth by an enquiry in 1744, while Drogheda had three diocesans in its two parishes and thirteen friars in three friaries. What is more important is that, by and large, the priests in the towns would seem to have been better equipped to preach and instruct both the general body of Catholics and the more educated middle classes. When John Donnelly, superior of the Dominicans at Drogheda, died in 1748, he had put together 164 works, mostly of French Jesuit theology, of a practical and homiletic rather than a speculative bent. John Wickham, parish priest of Templcshannon (Enniscorthy) died in 1777 leaving a library of 100 works in 260 volumes, again mostly practical theology, deriving in the main from Louvain where he had been educated, but with some indications of literary interests.[9]

In Wexford the friars and parish clergy had to share the same church, for Bishop Luke Wadding's chapel built inside the walls in the 1670s had fallen down and could not be replaced. At times this situation gave rise to tensions that generated a correspondence. Enough of it has survived to provide detail of the religious services at mid-century.[10] There were six priests in the town, three Franciscans, the bishop, Nicholas Sweetman, his assistant, and a young priest who 'yet got no parish' but helped out. There were six public Masses on Sundays and three on weekdays. On Sundays there was sung vespers. The bishop wished that they should always be of the Sunday (at that time the liturgy of a saint frequently took precedence over the Sunday one), so that the congregation could follow more intelligently – 'the laity have them in their manuals and are best accustomed to them' (sung vespers and benediction were regular Sunday services in the towns of the diocese of Cloyne in 1775). As in Dublin, so in Wexford the bishop did not approve of some of the friars' devotions: he thought they gave benediction too frequently and tried to prevent the parish clergy giving it at all, and in 1759 he was still trying to get the friars to take down the stations of the cross they had put up thirteen years before. Passing references in his examination in Dublin in 1751 indicate that this religious life, in so many ways open and organised, was still shadowed by the penal code: the Established Church still collected its fees for the parish sacraments, and there were at least symbolic limits to Catholic worship. No bell called the people together, he had to assure his questioners: 'never rings a bell but at the altar'.

Galway is interesting, and we are reasonably well informed about it. Surrounded by the unplanted counties, it had not been greatly affected by the Cromwellian policy of clearing the towns of Catholics, and it had shared the assurances given to the still unconquered areas by the treaty of Limerick. While civic authority was in the hands of Protestants, they were so few in number that they were barely able to sustain the necessary apparatus of the law (it was a waste of time arraigning a priest before Catholic jurors). Naturally, trade declined, despite smuggling, but the small nervous Protestant community could do little to curb Catholic practice. The most detailed information comes from an unusual source. Catholic missionaries had been expelled from China in 1707. One Italian group took passage to Europe in an English ship. They were weatherbound for months off the west coast of Ireland and spent some time in Galway. On his arrival in Rome one of them sent a long report to the pope that ended up in the archives of Propaganda.[11] The Catholics of Galway, he said, professed their faith openly in the face of threats and hardships; they kept fast and abstinence rigorously; they went outside the city to be able to attend Mass on Sunday, though there were secret oratories in the city where Mass was said, especially on Christmas night, when no one could leave because the gates were closed. When they heard there was a bishop on board they insisted on coming out to get his blessing, though threatened with punishment if they did, telling the Italian missionaries: 'We are Romans and afraid of nothing'.

The general enquiry of 1731 gave special attention to Galway. It did not prove easy to put the Catholic citizens on oath, or to force them to be specific in their answers, but it was established that there were nine secular priests, three friaries, a Jesuit, three 'nunneries which the papists commonly call boarding schools' and eight schoolmasters. It was not just the papists who were reluctant to provide information. The two city sheriffs reported to the mayor that they had searched the 'reputed friary in Back Street, but could not find or discover any of the said friars', tongue-in-cheek, for the surviving account-book of the Augustinian friary in Back Street records on 9 November 1731 'a bottle of wine for the sheriffs, 1s 1d', while the Dominicans noted spending 2s 2d 'for claret to treat the sheriffs in their search'.[12] If they called to the Franciscans and the nuns on the same day they might well have had trouble finding the last house on their list. 'No sham searches, Mr sheriffs', thundered Stratford Eyre, appointed governor of Galway two years later, 'as to my knowledge you have lately made. Your birds were flown, but they left you cakes and wine to entertain yourselves withal',[13] but though he carried on a long war against 'popish ecclesiastics' it was like trying to keep out the tide.

The story was very much the same in the unplanted counties of Connacht,[14] with which Clare may be included. Many of the Catholic gentry had survived the Cromwellian confiscation and had been protected by the articles of Limerick. Among them were descendants of Galway merchants who had acquired land in the sixteenth and seventeenth centuries, of Elizabethan settlers like the Brownes who had turned Catholic, and of families transplanted from other provinces, like the Bellews. Many conformed in the second half of the century, in fear of the gavel act or the discoverer, but relations between Catholic and Protestant appear to have remained good, though Catholic gentry, like Charles O'Conor of Belanagare, were very conscious of how precariously they held on to their lands. The better lands were extensively given over to grazing, and here the population was low and possibly declining. There were few roads, especially in the west, and at all levels society appears to have been isolated and clannish, little affected by outside developments. Here especially the old proprietors were held in esteem, whether they still held their lands or whether they had lost them, like the O'Donnell families, one of them, Hugh O'Donnell of Larkfield, Co. Leitrim, a descendant of Niall Garbh, now a tenant farmer, but commonly called 'the earl'. Foundations made in the Irish college in Paris evoke the same society: that of David Flyn, a priest of Tuam, in 1754, in favour first of his family, then of those of his name, then of 'anyone nominated by the chief of the O'Flyns or O'Conors', or that in 1761 in favour of 'Murry of Co. Clare ... descendants of all families who came from Ulster to Clare in Cromwell's time or since ... families translated from Ulster to Co. Mayo and borders of Sligo and Roscommon with preference for Murrys, O'Dohertys ...'.[15]

For the first half of the century the Catholicism of Connacht can be observed only from the outside, in the Public Record Office documents published by Burke and in the 1731 Report on the State of Popery.[16] They show considerable harassment during the worst years – an isolated item in the Flanders nunciature papers for December 1709 depicts the bishop of Elphin living 'in a kind of hut on a hillside', too poor to have a servant or a horse, paying someone to bring him the water he is too infirm to fetch for himself, admitting that he can get milk, but would dearly like a little beer.[17] Yet this harassment proved ineffective: as William Smith, the mayor of Sligo, wrote on 29 October 1714, 'the papists are so numerous in this county that without the assistance of the army there is no good to be done'. It was easier in Connacht than elsewhere for the Catholic Church to come through.

The framework of its structures may be seen with sufficient accuracy in the Report of 1731. Over the province, the Mass-house is the rule, and where, exceptionally, there is no Mass-house, only 'altars built of turf but not fixed', this seems to be the result of poverty rather than of the efforts of the magistracy. It is clear that the friars are numerous and influential, and that in many places they are living in some kind of community; and everywhere there are schools, one in almost every parish — 'a school almost in every two or three villages', it was noted of remote Erris, 'in so much that a Protestant schoolmaster where to be had can hardly get bread'.

A number of documents in the third quarter of the century allow a look at the church from the inside — diocesan statutes for Achonry (1759); diocesan reports on Elphin (1753, 1770), Tuam (1770) and Killala (1771) and ten letters written to Rome by a young priest, James Lyons, just returned to Ireland, between 1763 and 1765.[18] These sources complement one another, in the sense that the bishop in drawing up statutes has an eye on his clergy and will probably mention problems that although they may exist are rare, whereas in his reports to the congregation of Propaganda in Rome he will stress that they do not arise often; while the young priest may be presumed to report the situation, at least as he sees it, though naturally he too will be anxious to call attention to his own zeal.

The picture that emerges is that of a stable parish system, though in Killala in 1771 it was noted that there were still three parishes where the landlord would not allow a Mass-house to be built. There were regular deanery conferences to ensure that the clergy had the basic knowledge to instruct their people, but the indications are that the instruction they offered was more regularly in the form of catechesis rather than of a sermon, that it often took the form of catechising the children in the presence of the congregation either before or after Sunday Mass, and that some adults remained in ignorance even of very basic matters because they came for Mass only, and not for the catechesis. It is implied that attendance at Sunday Mass is good, because it is contrasted with the poor attendance, indeed non-attendance, on holydays. In 1755 Pope Benedict XIV had removed the obligation of abstaining from servile work on nineteen holydays, but had retained the obligation of going to Mass. In a thinly-populated countryside it was possible to go to Mass or to go to work, but not to do both, and the papal ruling seems to have endangered the observance of all holydays. At the request of many Irish bishops, the list of holydays was further shortened in 1778, and all obligations removed on the days that had been suppressed.

It is interesting that the bishops, when noting that some of the wealthy conform to the Established Church, invariably balance this by referring to conversions among the poor, though there is no suggestion that large numbers are involved, and it possibly means no more than that priests in the ordinary course of their work regularly bring people to an observance of the basic duties, Easter communion or even Sunday Mass (from other parts of the country there are indications that some of the poorer people – though again not many – may have been drawn into the Established Church in the early decades of the century). As noted above, it is only by implication that one can conclude that Sunday Mass attendance was on the whole good, but the implication seems rather firm. Similarly, the advice given to the priests of Achonry to get help for the Christmas and Easter confessions would, at least on the surface, seem to imply large numbers while in no way providing a percentage. James Lyons, while working in Dublin, reported 'many who have not approached the holy sacraments these three, four, eleven, sixteen, and twenty years'. He is not so specific when speaking of his native Sligo, but he does note that the decline in the numbers of the friars has led to an overall scarcity of priests. There are suggestions, too, that there may have been a problem with regard to the Irish language: Lyons confesses to a 'deficiency in my native language, which for the greater part I forgot in the college', and in 1748 an Irish Franciscan wrote from London that he regularly heard the confessions of Irish migrant labourers in the chapel at Lincoln's Inn Fields, 'ten Irish for one English confession . . . I have met with numbers who had not been for years together for want of an Irish confessor',[19] though these were more likely to have come from Munster and Leinster than from Connacht.

'The Catholics are docile and well disposed', Lyons wrote from Sligo in January 1765, 'and there would not be better in the world if oaths and drunkenness were not their second nature and essence'. In the towns, attempts had been made to deal with these problems by establishing confraternities, but these were not practicable in thinly-populated rural parishes. All in all, only an impressionistic picture of Connacht Catholicism in the eighteenth century is possible. The tridentine structure is there, and it is working towards effective catechesis, Sunday Mass and Easter duty, with what appears a fair measure of success. Even within the province there must have been regional differences, but if overall quantification is difficult regional quantification is impossible. For Connacht especially, there is reason to believe that the decline in the numbers of the friars in the second half of the century led to a real shortage of clergy. In these same years there were the large scale defections of Catholic gentry. Yet there is an overall impression of a strongly conservative society, perhaps coming under the influence of outside ideas for the first time when refugees arrived from Ulster in the 1790s, with the real change coming when Humbert landed at Killala in August 1798.

If one reason for Connacht Catholics being conservative was because they had suffered comparatively little in the plantations, Ulster Catholics may have been conservative because they suffered so much. Over much of the province there was a sizeable Protestant population, but the large proportion of dissenters, mostly Presbyterian, were themselves severely harassed at the beginning of the century, and not always disposed to join the Established Church in harassing the Catholics. Nevertheless, the Catholics suffered severely. Attempts to evangelise them did take place, but few are recorded, and they were unsuccessful. The Catholic clergy of Ulster may as yet have been poorly equipped to catechise their people, but they had quite sufficient influence to discredit any Protestant evangelists. In the 1704 registration only nine of the 189 priests registered in the nine counties of Ulster had been ordained abroad, and even when allowance is made for the number who went abroad to study after ordination the general level of formal theological formation must have been quite low.

What we know of the Catholics' harassment is to be found in the newspapers and in the documents from the Public Record Office printed by Burke.[20] It was possible to observe rural Connacht during those years only through these sources. For Gaelic Catholic Ulster, however, there are two sources that describe the society from within. One is the historian of Fermanagh, John Dolan, who wrote about 1720. He describes the old 'rites of passage' set in the old world:[21]

> When they marry their sons and daughters, suppose their portion does not exceed £20, they think nothing of spending £4 or £5 in a common bottle in the field, the marriage-day; for most commonly their simple sort is married in a field, where, after the ceremony and articles of marriage are concluded, they sit down upon the green, placing their chiefest and clergy at one end and the rest of them in two rows ... They bury none

except a beggar without a good store of dram; and if the deceased be not of substance to order his burial solemnity, his friends and neighbours do meet and make a contribution among themselves to see him buried with credit, these inhabitants generally being so united in manners and customs that a poor cotter would sooner venture the ruin of his poor family before he could see his child christened without a good store of dram.

The second is a long report on the Ulster dioceses, with great detail on his own diocese of Clogher (counties Fermanagh and Monaghan), sent to Rome in 1714 by Bishop Hugh MacMahon. Hugh was the eldest of three brothers who were successively bishops of Clogher and archbishops of Armagh. Of ancient Gaelic stock, his father, Colla Dubh, was one of the minority with enough business acumen to prosper even in very bad times. Hugh, born in 1660, was brought up within the Gaelic tradition. In 1683 he went to Rome, enrolled in the Irish college, and was ordained in 1688. Times were disturbed in Ireland, and on his journey back he got no further than Flanders, where he remained until he was named bishop of Clogher in 1707. When he arrived in Ulster he was the only bishop there except the ageing Patrick Donnelly of Dromore.

His detailed and compassionate report on conditions in 1714[22] reflects the two influences that went to his making — the old society of Gaelic Ulster, shattered but still living, and the theology of the Roman schools and his life as a priest in the Catholic Netherlands. What seems to have struck him most of all in Clogher was the people's attachment to the Mass. They had to travel long distances because priests were few. Even these few priests were being hotly pursued because they had refused the oath of abjuration. The bishop gives graphic accounts of Mass at night, Mass with the priest's face veiled, or Mass said by the priest alone in a room with the congregation outside, so that if summoned and interrogated they could truthfully say they did not know who the priest was. People far away would kneel down and pray at the hour they knew Mass was beginning. There can be no doubt of the devotion, though questions might arise about its quality, measured by tridentine standards. The answers must be closely connected with the question of catechesis. Here the bishop is definite: in these bad years there could be no catechesis at all. Neither were there any Catholic schools, and this worried him greatly. He was worried too about marriage, though, it would appear, about the forbidden degrees of kindred rather than about indissolubility. Banns for all marriages had to be called in the Protestant church, and the fee fixed by law paid to the minister. With no Catholic parish system there must have been many marriages within the degrees forbidden by canon law in this tightly-knit kin society.

He gave a detailed description of the Lough Derg pilgrimage. Here, as might be expected, the new had scarcely impinged on the old. Though banned by name in the legislation of 1703 forbidding pilgrimages, this, the greatest of them, was never interfered with and continued to attract pilgrims from all over Ireland. There they went from the beginning of June to the end of August, staying nine days, making the 'stations' three times a day. Masses were being said from dawn to mid-day, with two or three sermons daily, punctuated by loud cries of repentance. The most hardened sinners were converted. On the ninth day the pilgrim made a general confession and received communion at dawn, and spent the next twenty-four hours fasting and keeping vigil in the cave, ending his pilgrimage next morning with three plunges in the lake. The only concession to the early eighteenth century was the bishop's anxiety for a renewal of the plenary indulgence granted by Pope Clement XI. This must have been very marginal to the whole experience, as tridentine catechesis was marginal. Yet the experience ran deep, the repentance was real, and it expressed itself in the reception of the sacraments. It recalls the penitent in Connacht in the 1660s, whose catechetical knowledge was slender indeed, but protested that these deep matters were beyond him and that all he wanted was absolution for his sins.

The Report of 1731[23] is not particularly detailed for some of the Ulster dioceses, but the general pattern is clear. The number of priests is adequate, if they are personally equipped for their ministry and have facilities for their ministration. Though nothing approaching quantification is possible (no one in Ulster in 1731 would wish to advertise that he was a friar) there can be no doubt that there were considerable numbers of friars around. As for the personal quality of the clergy, it has been seen that at this time it was not good overall, in the sense that large numbers had not been formed to be good parish priests on the tridentine model, and that in this respect Ulster had always been at a disadvantage compared to the other provinces. In Ulster too it was harder to set up a parish structure. It differs markedly from the other provinces in that here the Mass-house was the exception – nine in Derry, for example, or five in Down and Connor. Elsewhere, the Catholics had to content themselves with an altar in the fields, not always with a fixed site, and it was to take another generation before this situation began to improve notably; and while the pattern of parish life in Ireland did not centre on the church to the extent the Council of

Trent would have wished, the Mass-house was at least as important for catechesis as it was for Mass observance, possibly more important. Schools could not supply the deficiency for these too were few and scattered, and at least in some instances the schoolmasters were sufficiently harassed to have to keep moving from place to place. Finally, only a couple of Catholics owned any property, and this had long been the case. Beyond doubt, the penal code in all its aspects bore heaviest in Ulster.

Material for an inside look at Catholic life in Ulster in the second half of the century is scarce enough: a diocesan report from Kilmore (1750), brief diocesan regulations for Armagh (1761) and fuller diocesan statutes for Clogher (1789).[24] Bishop Lawrence Richardson had been appointed to Kilmore in 1747. His report in 1750 gives some indication that he was still at the 'new broom' stage – he claims to have abolished drinking at wakes, in which he was most certainly deceiving himself, and to have with great success set up the confraternity of the Holy Name in every parish in the diocese as a remedy against profanity, where it is reasonable to assume he was deceiving himself, for, as has been seen, it was felt impracticable to set up confraternities in rural parishes even in the more favourable conditions obtaining in Connacht. His suggestion that the diocese is organised in thirty-six parishes must then be taken with some reservations, and his claim to have established a regular system of clerical conferences must be measured against his statement that the Sunday instruction takes the form of catechesis, and that even at this level it is not always given. The brief Armagh regulations of 1761 show that here some of the problems Bishop Richardson believed he had abolished were still in existence, and it is also clear that Archbishop Blake was far from having a church in each parish.

His predecessor, Archbishop Michael O'Reilly (d. 1758), had made a notable contribution by his two catechisms, in English and Irish, that continued in use in the Ulster dioceses well into the nineteenth century. They contained an 'Abridgement of the faith to be said on Sundays at the parish Mass and in private families', and in Clogher in 1789 we find the bishop prescribing its recitation (in Dublin just about this time Archbishop Carpenter was drawing up a similar formula). Though there were still places in Clogher where there was no Mass-house, the catechetical situation was under much better control, with catechesis, sermon or homily at Mass on Sunday, and if it was sometimes omitted one might suspect indolence perhaps more than ignorance, and suspect too that the conference-system may be working better than it was in

Kilmore forty years before. There are indeed problems with their roots in the old society: clandestine marriages, it may be presumed because of the forbidden degrees; abuses at wakes, including drunkenness; and drunkenness itself common among clergy as well as laity, and a particular scandal on Sundays and holydays. The old and the new still mingle, but these Clogher statutes indicate that the new is making some advances. By this time too relations between Catholics and Protestants had improved very much. Protestants were prepared to countenance the building of Catholic churches, and frequently contributed to the cost. In 1784 the Belfast Volunteers company 'paraded in full dress and marched to Mass, where a sermon was preached by the Rev. Mr O'Connell, and a handsome collection was made to aid in defraying the expense of erecting the new Mass-house. Great numbers of the other Protestant inhabitants also attended'.[25]

The rural areas of Leinster and Munster may be considered as a unit, with due allowance for regional variations over so wide an area. Nevertheless, there is a great deal of homogeneity. The two provinces contained the greater part of the good land of Ireland, and enjoyed the kinder half of its climate. Naturally, there were areas of poverty, associated with mountain and bogland. There were places very remote from government or indeed from any public authority, like the O'Connell territory at Derrynane. The two provinces had had a rather similar experience in the land confiscations. Catholics had held two-thirds of the land in them before 1641. At the end of the reign of Charles II they held about one-fifth. A number were restored in the old Pale, men of unimpeachable loyalty whose lands were in a safe area close to Dublin. Many won restoration under the patronage of the duke of Ormond, several Catholic Butlers in Kilkenny and Tipperary, and his brother-in-law the earl of Clancarty in Cork. They survived the Ormond attainder after 1715, but numbers conformed in the eighteenth century, among them the Catholic heir to the Ormond title, Walter Butler of Garryricken, who made his recantation of the errors of popery on 16 December 1764. Numbers survived, however, by one device or another, sometimes by good fortune, like the earls of Kenmare, who in two successive generations escaped the gavel act by producing only one son.

There were other Catholics of reasonable substance, fairly extensive graziers in the cattle-country, and, especially in the dairying districts of Munster, prosperous middlemen. These latter are the society reflected in Munster eighteenth-century poetry: it has been convincingly shown that Daniel Corkery's 'hidden Ireland' of the 'big house' in a sea of undifferentiated poverty is quite unreal.[26] A detailed examination of those who went surety for the registered clergy at £50 a time in 1704 should be very revealing – not just of the multiple guarantors, like Dudley Colclough of Mohurry in Co. Wexford, surety for eight priests, or John Browne of the Neale in Co. Mayo, surety for seven, both descendants of Elizabethan settlers, but perhaps more especially of those who went surety for one priest only. What is also clear is that the descendants of the dispossessed proprietors were held in respect even when reduced to poverty. Ferns diocesan statutes of 1722 recommend them as objects of charity, and Arthur Young in 1776 noted that the memory of their former estate had not faded, 'insomuch', he noted in Cork, 'that a gentleman's labourer will regularly leave to his son, by will, his master's estate'.[27] The leaders in 1798 in Wexford may be grouped in three classes: the liberal landlords, the Catholic priests, and the descendants of former proprietors, like Thomas Cloney of Moneyhore, Michael Furlong of Templescoby, or Edward Roche of Garrylough. The pattern is continuous from the 1660s – the landlord, the priest and the dispossessed.

As in the other provinces, priests suffered considerable harassment in Leinster and Munster in the years after 1709,[28] though, here as elsewhere, there is evidence of local magistrates unwilling to enforce the law, either because they thought the oath of abjuration unreasonable or because they were afraid. They had some reason to fear, for even in the more settled areas a mob outraged by the capture of a priest could be dangerous, as in documented instances at Cashel in 1714 and Carlow in 1739. Nevertheless, many priests were arrested, and many lay-people summoned and interrogated by the magistrates. No one was safe. In 1709 the earl of Kenmare had to write to Dublin to forestall an informer:[29]

> The priest of the parish said Mass in this cottage in an outward room. I was at it in an inward room with half a score more than tolerably pretty ladies and gentlemen among whom were at the fag end of the Mass a Protestant or two as God would have it. Mass being ended the door was shut against the congregation and we within fell to eating a breakfast of sheep and lamb's puddings ánd other rural things, and drank my lord lieutenant's health withal.

Here as elsewhere the Church organisation weathered the storm. The 1731 Report on the State of Popery [30] shows that by this date the Mass-house was far more common than the 'altar in the fields', though these did exist widely, at Inchigeelah, for example, 'no Mass-house, only a shade over the priest, the people standing in the open air', while of the Mass-houses it could be said that they were 'generally mean thatched cabins, many, or most of them, open at one end'. What decided between a Mass-house and a Mass-rock was normally the attitude of the landlord.

A few surviving diocesan regulations[31] from the earlier years of the century give some indication of how things were kept going. The parish framework afforded by the 1704 Registration Act was maintained. In Ferns in 1722 it was a bit ragged at the edges, but it was noticeably firmer in Dublin in 1730. The bishop's control over the nomination of parish priests was not altogether complete. There were some, apparently, who were not diocesans, and who felt free to go if they wished. At times, too, the bishop's rights seem to be resisted because he will not accept that the simple fact of possession constitutes a right to a parish, and more frequently because laymen claim rights, in some instances the landlords who permitted a Mass-house, Protestants as well as Catholics. Priests were known to appeal to Protestant magistrates against a bishop's decision. On the whole, however, there was a fair measure of conformity to tridentine discipline: the counties of the south and east, with their regular trading links with Europe, always had a larger proportion of priests with a continental seminary education. In consequence, they were better equipped for catechesis, but even here in these years what was expected of them was limited. Some priests did preach, but what was expected of all was less demanding. In Ferns in 1722 a summary of faith and morals according to the prescribed diocesan formula was to be recited at Sunday Mass if no other instruction was given. The priest was expected to catechise the people in the houses where he lodged. There was to be catechism for the children on Sundays, and there are indications that a share in this work was already devolving on the schoolmaster.

In regard to penance, so closely related to catechesis, we are dealing with indications rather than with firm evidence. There is a clear concern that people be sufficiently instructed to discharge the paschal precept, and a Dublin regulation in 1730 insisting that the parish priest be personally available for confessions on Sunday mornings may indicate concern that the people have opportunity to confess. Concern is also expressed that people have the basic instruction regarded as necessary for marriage. Marriage and baptism, at least so the diocesan regulations would have it, are established as parish sacraments. There are some firm but cautious regulations about 'mixed' marriages between Catholics and Protestants in Ferns in 1722, though it cannot be concluded that these occurred in any way frequently. Neither can evidence be sought in parish registers, although every parish priest was ordered to keep them. Priests were reluctant to do this for many years to come, fearing that if persecution flared up they would provide evidence of their ministry. Very few eighteenth-century registers survive in the diocese of Ferns. After Wexford town, which goes back to 1671, the next earliest is Lady's Island, beginning in 1737.

The third of the 'rites of passage', wakes and funerals, continues to provide evidence of the survival of old customs. In Ferns the parish priests were ordered to spare no effort to end the practice of women keening at funerals, while in Dublin there was concern about immodest songs and games at wakes. There was concern too about various forms of superstition. That it was fairly widespread might be deduced from the fact that in Ferns in 1722 it was a reserved sin to practise the 'black arts', but not to consult those who practised them.

For the years after 1745 there is a wider range of sources[32] that allow of firmer conclusions, all the more so as Church life became less subject to disturbance, or even to the threat of disturbance, though fears understandably persisted. The anti-popery proclamation of 1744 was couched in terms of the Banishment Act, tacitly accepting the failure of the attempts to impose the oath of abjuration, and though the diocesan clergy were carefully listed there seems to have been little attempt to interfere with their ministry once the Jacobite attempt of 1745 had failed, and, in particular, had led to no disturbance in Ireland.

The detailed Cashel diocesan visitations of the 1750s and the brief but informative Ferns visitation of 1753 show the parish system firmly established. Every parish has its Mass-house, though sometimes a second Mass on Sundays has to be provided at a 'station' in another part of the parish. At times, inevitably, the bishop on visitation has to deal with problems, but the overall impression is certainly of a system that is working well. The Sunday Mass was also the principal occasion for instruction. The deanery clerical conferences, struggling earlier in the century, were now firmly established, though the Dominican Bishop Troy of Ossory, appointed in 1776, noted that they had lapsed for several years under his predecessor, Thomas de Burgo, also a Dominican. In the second half of the century there was less and less to supplement the parish's own resources. There had been some attempt at parish missions, especially by the Jesuits, in the easier days of the early seventeenth century. At the beginning of the eighteenth there were only sporadic attempts by the friars. The friars were not always welcome, because of the strained relations between the diocesan and regular clergy, and it would appear that at times there was reason why they should not be welcome, for they were on a thinly disguised quest rather than on anything that might be described as a parish mission. After 1750 the numbers of the friars declined rapidly, and the parish mission seems to have altogether disappeared.

The minimum the archbishop of Cashel demanded of his clergy was that they possess the constitutions, *prône* and catechism of the diocese. The *prône* or book of prepared sermons in the French tradition seems to have been widely used in the Munster dioceses especially, but so far there has been no attempt to evaluate its contribution to the overall catechesis. The catechism was still the standby, though the number of priests able to preach was steadily increasing. In Ossory in 1769 it would appear that not all were capable of preaching, but in Cloyne six years later the bishop noted that the Sunday sermon was now the rule, and that only a few of the older priests who were unable to preach were still alive. The problem remained of the priest who did not preach, not because he was unable, but because he would not take the trouble, like John Fitzhenry in Ferns in 1753, noted by the sharp eye of his bishop as 'an honest indolent man, who neither preaches nor teaches his flock'.[33]

The Cashel visitations, supported in less detail from other sources, indicate that the catechesis of children had devolved more and more on the schoolmaster and on candidates for the priesthood, who were often schoolmasters themselves. Earlier in the century there had been few Catholic schools, and in these years some of the poor especially seem to have been willing to send their children to Protestant schools to learn the rudiments, where some of them were absorbed into the Protestant Church. Catholic sources later in the century regularly report that although there have been a few defections among the better off greater numbers of the poor have been converted. Numbers are not always given, and when given they need careful interpretation. For example, the 370 conversions over four years noted in Cloyne in 1775 must certainly include the return to the Catholic Church of a number of people who for various reasons connected with the Whiteboy disturbances had made a brief sojourn in the Church of Ireland, where, it would appear, most if not all of them were unwelcome.

Catholic schools developed rapidly after 1733 to counter what was regarded as the serious threat of the Charter schools; and there is enough evidence from other sources to allow the detailed account of the situation in Cashel to be regarded as fairly typical. Cashel in the 1750s had at least 73 schoolmasters teaching catechism. Cloyne in 1775 had 117. It has already been noted that Dublin in 1787 had 40 parish schools with 1770 pupils, while Ferns in 1796 had schools in each parish, under the direction of the parish priest. It is possible to follow the working of the system in detail in Cashel at mid-century, and it is quite clearly a parish system. In three instances it is explicitly stated that school was held in the Mass-house, and it is reasonable to believe that this was the rule wherever it was necessary. It is very clear too that the archbishop regarded the schoolmaster as an object of his visitation equally with the parish priest. He was expected to teach the catechism. If he did not, he was carpeted: if he could not, he was instructed. Unfortunately, there were parish priests, and doubtless bishops, who left this task to the schoolmaster and took less care than the archbishop of Cashel to see that he did it well.

That the overall catechesis was not satisfactory might be deduced from the consistent concern that a great number of people do not discharge the minimum requirement of the paschal precept of annual confession and communion. In 1769 Bishop de Burgo of Ossory felt that this was because there were not enough confessors, particularly because there were now fewer friars, but he himself was a Dominican, and in 1748 a predecessor, also a Dominican, was disturbed because a great many people had not fulfilled their paschal precept for a number of years. A similar situation may lie behind the regulation for Achonry in 1759 already noted that ordered parish priests to get assistance for the Christmas and Easter confessions because of the great numbers of penitents. This may mean that confession at Christmas and Easter was the rule, but it is possible too that all it means is that the numbers involved did put a strain on the services provided, and how good these were we do not know, except that it might be suspected that it was not always easy for the parish priest to get assistance. What proportion of the population did not fulfil the paschal precept cannot be established. Bishop Madgett of Kerry noted in 1753 that there were great crowds at communion in Tralee – perhaps significantly, on the feast of St John the Baptist, outside the obligatory period laid down by the Church – and in 1796 Bishop Caulfield reported that many in his diocese were at confession and communion every month, but the consistently expressed concern remains, that in this matter many people do not fulfil their minimum obligations.

Enough registers survive from the later years of the century to confirm the general impression that the administration of baptism had become routine. That it was normally administered in the home is clear, for example, from the absence of any reference to baptismal fonts in descriptions of the chapels, though this practice may have changed as the chapels became better: in Cloyne in 1786 it was 'generally performed at the chapels or in priests' houses'.[34] In the matter of marriage and sexual morals, it would appear that a pattern of pre-marital continence with a growing tendency to early marriage was well on the way to being established by mid-century. The 'made match' is standard in the middle-class society described by the Munster poets. When the poet wants to protest that he really loves the girl the phrase that comes to his lips is that he would marry her if she had not a penny fortune. Brian Merriman was hardly conducting a social survey: one might well suspect that his principal source was 'pub-talk', inspired pub-talk indeed, but pub-talk none the less. The detailed Cashel visitations of the 1750s are particularly valuable here. Public repentance is demanded of sexual offenders, men as well as women. There is indeed one character wandering through these visitations who could have delighted Merriman, but only one, and he is so diligently pursued by the clergy that he must have been exceptional. And while the clergy do keep a sharp eye out for sexual offenders they are equally concerned with other things. Archbishop Butler's more routine enquiries tend to be about catechesis, superstitions, or the widespread habit of blasphemy. What the Church authorities are most concerned with in regard to marriage is the problem of clandestinity, that is, marriages not celebrated by the parish priest or his delegate. There were many reasons for clandestine marriages. One was an unwillingness to pay the fee demanded by the parish priest. Again, for one reason or another there may have been a desire to keep the marriage secret, especially if it were a 'mixed' marriage. Other reasons arose from the fact that Church law had established various annulling impediments arising from relationships between the parties to be married. A dispensation could be got in many of them, but not in certain degrees of relationship, to an extent that was genuinely irksome in what was still a closely-knit kin society. If a dispensation were granted there was a fee to the bishop. Many people wished to have a dispensation from the formal calling of the banns of marriage. Marriages not celebrated by the parish priest were not canonically invalid on that head alone except where the *Tametsi* decree of Trent had been duly promulgated – in 1678 in the province of Armagh, in Tuam (except Galway) in 1745, in Cashel in 1775 and in Dublin and Galway only in 1827. Marriages within certain degrees of relationship were invalid in the eyes of the Church but valid in civil law. There was then plenty of scope for 'Tack 'em', the couple-beggar. He offered a more flexible service and in some cases a cheaper one.

By mid-century the Catholic parish system had been established in a recognisably modern form. No other conclusion is possible from a reading of the Cashel visitations. More strictly statistical evidence is scanty, though what remains of the religious census of 1766 might go some way to answer questions, especially for those parishes where, exceptionally at this date, parish registers survive for the Catholic Church or the Church of Ireland, or, better still, for both. The census was made at a time when the establishment was greatly worried by the Whiteboy disturbances, which it wished to represent as the activities of disloyal papists. On this head, it is unlikely that the number of Catholics was underestimated. However, the enumeration was entrusted to the tithe-proctors, and it is probable that at least in some instances they may have missed some of the real poor who paid no tithes. It is likewise a reasonable assumption that most of these were Catholics. The census, then, may be accepted as accurate within the resources available at the time, with perhaps a slight propensity to underestimate Catholic numbers.

The census returns were lost in the destruction of the Public Record Office. Nothing survives except partial copies and summaries made by Tenison Groves. The example which follows is offered more to raise questions than to suggest answers. His summaries for the dioceses of Kilmore and Ardagh are conveniently available in print.[35] The two dioceses correspond very closely with the three counties of Cavan, Leitrim and Longford. These counties may be regarded as a fair sample, being in three different civil provinces and having had different experiences of plantation. The 1766 figures for each county may be compared with the corresponding figures for 1861, the first nineteenth-century census to distinguish religious affiliations (the figures for 1766 are based on an enumeration of families, these of 1861 on an enumeration of individuals):

		Catholics	Protestants
Cavan	1766	77.3%	22.7%
	1861	80.5%	19.5%
Leitrim	1766	86%	14%
	1861	89.8%	10.2%
Longford	1766	87.5%	12.5%
	1861	90.4%	9.6%

These figures obviously represent the beginnings of research, not its conclusions, but they do suggest that over a hundred years the religious affiliations may not have changed significantly.

Shortly after mid-century there is indeed a certain sense of stability. There is a degree of ease in the relations between Catholics and Protestants, and relations continue to be good in many respects for the next few decades, Catholics and Protestants attending one another's funerals, for example, or Protestants contributing to the building of Catholic chapels. Yet the whole system made for tensions. In particular, Protestants never lost the fear of an overthrow of the settlement, as was shown in the reaction to the Whiteboy disturbances, and Catholics never lost the fear that active persecution might come again. That they were not without reasons for their fear was shown, for instance, by the arrest and interrogation of Bishop Sweetman of Ferns in 1751 on a charge of being a Jacobite agent brought against him by a drunken and incorrigible priest (it would be hard to deduce that such a thing could happen from the bishop's account of his diocesan visitation a short time later, in 1753). As late as 1781 Lord Doneraile closed every Mass-house on his estate. A parish priest had declared excommunicated a parishioner long living in open adultery. Lord Doneraile ordered him to lift the excommunication, and when the priest said he could not Lord Doneraile horsewhipped, kicked and beat almost to death the old man of eighty-one and his aged housekeeper. He was tried for assault and £1,000 damages awarded against him. In one sense this was, as Thomas Davis called it, 'the first spoils of emancipation',[36] but the immediate consequence was the closing of every Mass-house on the Doneraile estate.

Now we must approach directly the key question, the quality of religious life in the Catholic community. In some sense the Mass and the Mass-house is certainly at its centre. It is not possible to dismiss simply as an indication of the clerical propensity for building that consistent feeling earlier in the century that the tangible sign of progress is the provision of a Mass-house, and, in its later years, the provision of a 'chapel' where some dignity of worship was possible, like those of Tralee and Killarney, better than any Protestant church in the diocese, as Bishop Moylan claimed in 1785, or of Limerick, where, at a charity sermon for schools in 1793, the chapel 'was brim full of Protestants, clergy and laity' and there was a 'fine band of music, mostly gentlemen'.[37] By the closing decades of the eighteenth century the Mass-house in Ireland had come to discharge much of the role the Council of Trent had envisaged for the parish church.

While the historian may be interested in seeing Protestants and Catholics together in the chapel on occasion, interested too in the 'band of music', especially perhaps those who were not gentlemen, for him the important question is how many attended Sunday Mass? In this matter we have no statistics for the eighteenth century. The earliest available date from 1834, and as they have been the subject of some study recently by the American historians Emmet Larkin and David W. Miller[38] it may not be altogether irrelevant to take them into account here. Miller in particular comes up with some detailed statistical analysis, though, as he says, the figures available are in many cases subject to more than one interpretation and in no sense represent a modern socio-religious study. On the basis of sampling in areas where the figures seem firmest, he concludes that Mass attendance figures were: the four biggest cities (Dublin, Cork, Belfast, Limerick), 40 per cent to 60 per cent; the other towns, 80 per cent to 100 per cent; the rural English-speaking areas, 30 per cent to 60 per cent; and the rural Irish-speaking areas 20 per cent to 40 per cent. A few comments on his method seem worth making, two in particular. One is that where the information given is open to more than one interpretation he chooses the lower figure. The second is that he makes no allowance for those not bound to hear Mass, especially the children under seven. These he should quite certainly have excluded. The annual *Catholic Directory,* beginning in 1836, has in its earlier issues a list of rules for 'Conduct in the house of God'. The sixth reads: 'Mothers should take care not to disturb the congregation by bringing children under the age required'. Children under seven amounted to one-sixth of the population. If we add the aged, the sick, the otherwise impeded – mothers caring for young children, for example – it is a conservative estimate that one-fifth of the total population did not come to Mass because the precept of attending did not bind them. Correcting Miller's figures by this factor, we get: the four cities, 50 per cent to 75 per cent; the other towns, effectively 100 per cent; the rural English-speaking areas, 37.5 per cent to 75 per cent; and the rural Irish-speaking areas, 25 per cent to 50 per cent. These figures must be regarded as minimum figures rather than as firm figures, because of Miller's opting for the lower percentage where his data are ambiguous. They are still far from the universal 100 per cent attendance regarded as traditional in Irish Catholicism, and they do fall into a pattern closely corresponding to the pattern of conscious commitment to Counter-reformation religious practice discernible in Ireland since early in the seventeenth century. Do they also correspond to the actual figures for Mass-attendance in the second half of the eighteenth? There are reasons for thinking that they do not.

  Concern is regularly expressed over a number of pastoral problems in eighteenth-century Ireland, but Sunday Mass-attendance is never mentioned as one of them. What is mentioned, particularly in the western dioceses, is the problem arising between 1755 and 1778 from the fact that on a number of holydays there is an obligation to attend Mass but not to refrain from work. On these days most people do not attend Mass, because if they go to work they have no time to go to Mass. By implication – and sometimes the implication rides almost to the level of assertion – there is no such problem on Sundays. Neither is there any indication that Mass at the 'stations of confession' in houses throughout the parish was widely accepted as fulfilling the Sunday precept. It is quite difficult to trace the origin of these 'stations'. There is evidence through the century of concern that the people may not have sufficient opportunities of going to confession, and the 'stations' are firmly established in the Munster dioceses by 1786,[39] where they are one of the issues the provincial bishops deal with in answer to the complaints of the Whiteboys that too much is being charged by the priests for their ministrations. Another line of evidence emerges from complaints about how Catholics observe the Sabbath: for example, a description of a Sunday football match near Rathfarnham in 1789 that ended in 'much bloodshed and battery' prompts the comment that the influence of the Catholic clergy over their people is so strong 'that scarcely even the most profligate of them will dare to be absent from divine worship on Sunday'.[40] It seems reasonable to conclude that in this matter things got worse as times got harder, especially in the poorer areas that in the early nineteenth century developed into a disaster waiting to happen.

The evidence for the quality of participation at Mass is scarce, and the usual class and regional variations may be expected. Active participation may be presumed with the middle-class, especially in the towns, following Mass and vespers from their manuals. Bishop Plunkett's notes on his 1780 visitation of Meath indicate problems in the country districts – 'lack of respect due to the house of God; for they spoke and were otherwise very dissipated during Mass', and, echoing older ways, 'the custom that prevails among the women of shouting and groaning at every word the priest says with emphasis'.[41]

After the Mass came devotion to Our Lady, especially the rosary. Piaras Mac Gearailt, forced to conform early in the century, found the absence of devotion to Mary the most distasteful aspect of 'the Saxon Lutheran religion'. Everywhere 'the beads is duly observed by most of the people', Archbishop Butler noted during his visitations. In Dublin at mid-century it was claimed that even some Protestants secretly carried rosaries in their pockets. If they did, they were probably well advised to keep them there, for in Protestant eyes generally the rosary was a kind of talisman of popery and Jacobitism: when the Young Pretender was burnt in effigy in Youghal in 1745 he had 'a bundle of rosaries (or padareens) hung to his nose, to show his obedience to the pope'.[42] As already noted, the catechism was the mainstay of religious instruction. A good demand created a good supply. The eighteenth century saw substantial additions to the catechetical inheritance of the seventeenth, notably the catechisms of Archbishop O'Reilly and of Andrew Donlevy, both of them in English and Irish versions, the former especially having very wide popularity, possibly because it was shorter. To these might be added English imports, especially Mannock's *The Poor Man's Catechism,* and an abridgement of Turberville's (the 'Douai catechism') of 1645, which also kept its popularity. All these catechisms were in the Jesuit tradition, stressing obedience to the positive commands of Church authority, regular Mass-attendance and regular prayers and devotions. They were, of course, learned by rote, but they contained many texts of prayers and 'acts', thereby keeping a balance between intellectual understanding of one's religion and living it which was unfortunately lost when 'Butler's catechism' of the 1770s left little or nothing except question and answer.[43]

It has been seen too that the duty of catechising children tended to devolve on the schoolmaster. The results were not altogether happy, and the fault lay, not with the schoolmaster, but with the priest, who left the job to the schoolmaster and in many cases took insufficient care to see that he did it properly. That at least is the verdict of Bishop Plunkett of Meath in his visitation of 1780. Almost everywhere he went he noted that, though the children generally knew the catechism, they answered 'like parrots', from rote memory and not understanding what they said.

The growth of a Catholic reading public has already been discussed in connection with the urban middle-classes. The growth of habits of reading among the more prosperous in the countryside is not so easily evaluated. Not all were drunken squireens: the family of the future Cardinal Cullen might be instanced as one that certainly was not. Apart from the catechisms, printed material in the Irish language was very scarce indeed. There seems to have been a kind of positive reluctance to abandon the manuscript tradition for the printing press. Bishop Gallagher's *Sixteen Irish Sermons in an Easy and Familiar Stile* (1736) met an obvious need, but he had no successors. The manuscript texts were multiplied with dogged determination under worsening conditions, but it does seem strange to see eighteenth-century scribes copying manuscript texts printed by the Louvain Franciscans in the seventeenth. The religious texts they copy are translations, of continental origin, not English, but here as in the printed book in English there is little to nourish a native spirituality. One might venture a guess that the manuscript tradition influenced Gaelic society more widely than did the printed book in English, but in all this field there is much we do not know. What, for instance, was the influence of Tadhg Gaelach Ó Súilleabháin? He turned exclusively to religious themes in middle age, and after his poems were printed (the first edition in Clonmel in 1802) they enjoyed very great popularity.

The role of the priest was changing with the changing times. When a layman conformed to the Established Church the reaction of his neighbours was a wry shrug of the shoulders – he had acted to save his property. It was different in the case of a priest. The conforming priest was attacked in some very bitter poetry, mockingly bitter if he married, savagely bitter if he exercised orders in the Established Church. On the whole, relations between the poets and priests were good. There are many poems in praise of priests, though the themes are stereotyped and personal details are scanty. There are criticisms too, of incontinence sometimes, but more often of avarice and ignorance. Yet these criticisms, with the biting criticism of priests who conform, do not necessarily imply a wide-spread acceptance of the tridentine ideal of the priesthood. In many ways the priest is still the 'man of power'. Before the Reformation he had shared power especially with the *file* and the *breitheamh*. As their offices decayed it was only natural that more of their powers should pass to the priest. Perhaps it might even be said that he inherited some of the powers of the *taoiseach,* and that while this made him loved and respected it also made him feared.[44] The Rightboy disturbances in Munster and Kilkenny in the 1780s revealed a resentment against some of the Catholic clergy because of their exactions in the matter of dues and fees sufficiently serious to cause real concern to the bishops. Bishop Plunkett on visitation in 1780 certainly believed that some of the priests were feared and not loved, harsh masters obviously disliked. As he wrote of one parish:[45]

> Those that were confirmed answered very well . . . many others answered well also; it was a pity they had not been to confession; hence they could not be confirmed. The very few that did not answer well would have answered better had they not been half frightened out of their wits by Father Bartle's thundering voice.

Examples like these strongly suggest that nineteenth-century comparisons between the domineering 'Maynooth priest' and his kindly predecessors from the continental colleges must be taken with some reservation. A somewhat similar distinction emerged after the Famine between the old landlords and the new harsh ones who had bought land under the Encumbered Estates Act. The past always takes on a golden glow.

How many were feared and how many were loved? Maybe all the historian can say is that this is known only to God. It may very well be that the effective exclusion of the friars from the pastoral mission removed a humanising influence, though some would – and did – consider it over-humanising. Through fear or love – or a judicious mixture – these priests had presided over the introduction of some of the ways of Counter-reformation spirituality. They had a real but limited success in catechetics and in the closely-related matter of penance. They had more success with Sunday Mass, with the sacraments of baptism and marriage, and in developing certain habits of prayer. (I have deliberately drawn back from the difficult question of relating the rich surviving heritage of traditional prayers in Irish to the estimates made by the bishops and clergy of their successes in this area, because here I have no competence at all. It must be very hard to relate this basically oral tradition to definite times and definite places, but its existence must always be taken into account in any assessment of the verdict of the clergy on how well the people pray.)

In some areas of life, however, not even the power of the priest was able to change much. One was the third 'rite of passage', death, wakes and funerals. Bishop Gallagher of Kildare in 1748 prohibited 'unchristian diversions of lewd songs, brutal tricks called fronsy-fronsy', at 'wakes and watches of the dead', and 'loud cries and howlings' at wakes and burials.[46] Accounts from other dioceses, Kilmore in 1750, for example, or Clogher in 1789, show the same problem. Indeed the clergy seem to have made some contribution to keeping old burial-customs alive, at least to the extent of encouraging the feasting and drinking associated with wakes and funerals by insisting on their own share.

Neither were they altogether innocent in regard to the superstitions that permeated the fact of life as well as the fact of death – Bishop Sweetman of Ferns in his diocesan regulations of 1771 found it necessary to include priests who 'act the fairy doctor' in his denunciation of superstitions.[47] Bishop Madgett of Kerry in 1760 declared it was impossible to root out these ancestral fears and usages however much the clergy preached against them, and he himself was not prepared to rule out altogether the power of sorcery, because of instances priests had given him. Madgett gives a detailed account of the prevalent superstitions that tallies closely with that given by Martin Marley in *The Good Confessor*:[48]

> Did you make use of any superstitions, or vain observations, persuading yourself that there are lucky and unlucky days: unlucky, if the first person you should meet in the morning should be red-haired, or if a hare should cross the way before you, or if a grave should be opened on a Tuesday, or if a marriage, or any bargain should be made on that day of the week, upon which Holy Innocents fell that year, or if thirteen should be at table etc., which are the remains of heathenism, vain and groundless remarks.
>   Did you make use of superstitious things for curing of diseases in men or cattle, which have, or can have, no natural connection with these effects, such as billets, certain words, prayers not approved by the Church, herbs gathered before sunrise, or on certain days only, a little stone, or flint-arrow dipped in milk, ale or water . . . had you recourse to magicians, sorcerers or witches?

He proposed this list in 1743 as useful for examination of conscience before confession. Some of the items on it had a long life ahead of them.

Another area where the Church made little impact was the widespread violence of word and action. Church denunciation of widespread profanity has already been noted in more than one context. The impact of the denunciation was limited: in his diocesan report of 1771 the bishop of Killala noted that people who knew no other word of the language could curse in English.[49] The last of the tories held out until late in the century: a noted tory died in Fermanagh in 1782. They perhaps provided the link between the aristocratic war-games and cattle-raids of former times and the popular violence so well established in the eighteenth century, to some extent the reaction of people whose only defence was the mob. Violence was endemic in the mean streets of Dublin. In the countryside, every gathering tended to end in violence. Indeed, said Bishop Troy of Ossory in 1782, people go there to get drunk and 'with the anti-Christian intention of raising a quarrel, or revenging a real or imaginary insult offered to their relations, friends and partisans.'[50] Ecclesiastical denunciation was steady, but ineffective. Bishop Moylan of Kerry was deceiving himself when he felt that clerical opposition would improve matters because the people would obey the clergy. In this area they would not obey them. The faction-fight was part of life well before the nineteenth-century police-records allow its documentation in detail.

There was another matter with directly religious origins that degenerated into superstition and violence, the traditional pilgrimages and patterns. The government wished to suppress them, fearing any gathering of papists, and legislation of 1703 had in fact done so. Like so much of the religious legislation of the penal code, this law was enforced only very sporadically even in the worst years after 1709 and even then mostly in the neighbourhood of Dublin. From the religious point of view, these pilgrimages had in the middle ages tended to be encrusted with the superstitions of popular religion. Especially in the earlier seventeenth century, the Counter-reformation clergy had made some effort to turn them into genuine festivals of Christian saints. As times got harder the effort seems to have slackened, and perhaps it never could have succeeded. Certainly by the closing decades of the eighteenth century the Church had set its face against the tradition of pilgrimage and pattern, and thereby helped to ensure that they would degenerate into 'meetings of pretended devotion, or rather of real dissipation and dissoluteness', to quote Bishop Sweetman of Ferns in 1771. In the words of his neighbour Bishop Troy of Ossory in 1782, 'they profane the name of God and everything else that is sacred by the most execrable oaths, and finish the day by the perpetration of the grossest impurities, by shedding their neighbour's blood, by murder, and the transgression of every law'.[51] There were priests, possibly in closer touch with their people, some of them possibly only to the extent of wishing to share their holiday, who went along to say Mass. We know this from the stringent rules laid down by the bishops to regulate the saying of Mass at pilgrimages and patterns. In the face of episcopal opposition the religious element in them withered.

The last few pages have presented the darker side of the story, the areas of religious concern where the Church had had small success in imposing its standards. Naturally, these should be balanced against those areas where it did succeed, and one must be careful not to construct too tidy a formula or model implying any kind of progressive advance. It may be that the real pattern contains elements of advance and retreat, territory won here and lost there. It may be too that areas were being lost or at least eroded in the second half of the eighteenth century. It has already been suggested that the standard of attendance at Sunday Mass may have declined in the fifty-odd years before the 1830s, especially in the poorer districts. But in important areas the Catholic Church of the penal era had succeeded in building a pattern of 'tridentine' religious observance. The success was not uniform: the pattern already discernible early in the seventeenth century does seem to run through, namely that there was a greater measure of success in the towns and with the better-off classes. But it would not be just to stress too exclusively the drunkenness, violence and supersitition in the societies furthest removed from the areas of greater success, in the 'the hidden Ireland'. Here too such things must be set against the successes achieved in religious observance. Here especially they were balanced by another factor, no less real because less quantifiable. In some respects 'the hidden Ireland' was a unique society. Its people were poor, and even for the better-off there was an element of uncertainty, but, especially in Gaelic Ireland, they treasured memories of a greater past. Here one thinks first perhaps of the music, especially the aristocratic harp-music, of interest to polite society now that James Macpherson had discovered Ossian, and preserved at the end of its days by Bunting and others. The scribal tradition had become antiquarianism, and the poetic strain tended to sink with the society it lived in, but these old tunes had a solemn beauty that inspired art-music from Beethoven to Seán Ó Riada, and proved itself able to survive words of unspeakable banality.

The much smaller 'hidden Ireland' that spoke English had no comparable aristocratic memories. For it I choose a ballad, obviously inspired by contemporary events but yet suggesting that its roots are in an old culture. That culture is hidden indeed, and can only prompt questions to which there are few answers. There are scattered clues – for example, the text of 'one of those old English ballads ... of the barony of Bargy' printed in 1867 by the Wexford antiquarian, Patrick Kennedy.[52] He says he had heard this ballad, 'Fair Eleanor', at a wake when he was young. It could have come straight out of Percy's *Reliques of Ancient English Poetry*. The ballad I have in mind here is better known: it is 'The Croppy Boy', not in the version too often heard, its words by a minor poetaster of the *Nation,* the language 'standard pseudo-peasant', sticky with cheap romanticism:

> Good men and true in this house who dwell
> To a stranger *bouchal* I bid you tell . . . ,

but the original ballad of the broadsheets:

> It was early, early in the spring
> When small birds tune and thrushes sing
> Changing their notes from tree to tree
> And the song they sang was old Ireland free,

with its spare and nervous language, its capacity in a few words to evoke a sense of place and occasion:

As I was going through Wexford street,
My own first cousin I there did meet,
My own first cousin did me betray
And for one guinea swore my life away.

There is a kind of whistle of doomed youth about it, *et mentem mortalia tangunt.*

6   Return to the Political Nation

The last chapter has attempted to study a society almost exclusively from its religious aspect, with some attention to social and regional differentiations within it that are too easily forgotten and that the national legend has tended to ignore. The aim has been to ascertain the pattern of religious life that had taken shape about 1760, though evidence from later in the century has been adduced wherever it was felt to be useful. There is inevitably a certain unreality about studying one aspect of life in isolation, though perhaps less than usual for the Irish Catholics in the first half of the eighteenth century, because there were not many other aspects to their lives. But about 1760 this society began to stir. Changing economic circumstances began to generate new pressures. The first prospects of a return to the political nation began to appear. The experiences of being an Irish Catholic began to broaden out, and this aspect of history must now be examined. It will involve to some extent going over rather well-trodden ground, though some themes, especially the important popular agrarian movements, have received fresh attention quite recently. An understanding of these is very important in estimating the pressures in the later decades of the century, pressures arising from the condition of the Irish Catholics, who seek admission to social and political life, and of those who have to grant that admission, 'the Protestant interest'.

Josiah Hort was the Protestant archbishop of Tuam during the forty-five. Apart perhaps from the fact that in early life he had conformed to the Established Church from Presbyterianism, his progress towards an Irish archbishopric was not untypical of the eighteenth century. He had arrived in Ireland in 1710 as chaplain to the lord lieutenant, a post well established as the first rung on the ladder of promotion. It had led Josiah Hort to the bishopric of Ferns in 1722, to Kilmore in 1727, and finally to his archbishopric in 1742. In the disturbed year of 1745 he had issued a pastoral charge to his clergy, as had a number of other prelates of the Established Church, but none revealed a mentality more clearly:

You will notice that I am not for inciting your people to act offensively

116

towards the Roman Catholics, for they have made ample professions and declarations of remaining quiet and amenable to the government at this time; and I would in charity hope that they are in good earnest; but however, it is the part of wisdom to guard against the worst, while we hope for the best; and I am sure they are best to be trusted when they see us prepare for our defence ... Your only course must be to visit them at their houses, and to show them by friendly reasonings where their true interest lies ... You may fairly ask them, if their persons and properties have not been in safety ever since they remained quiet and peaceable ... Do not their Protestant landlords and masters treat them as kindly as their popish ones? And, do not their poor receive more charity from Protestants than from those of their own religion? Penal laws have indeed been made against them, but chiefly against their priests, for the defence of the government against their dangerous principles and practices; but what do the bulk of the papists feel from these laws? ... Now, if these are all undeniable facts, what can any modest and reasonable papist desire more, and how can he be aggrieved?[1]

For most of the ascendancy for most of the time, 'it is remarkable how the members of this proud community were able to ignore the existence of their helots'[2], and at times of stress such as the forty-five they tried to reassure themselves that 'modest and reasonable papists' had no reason for discontent. Perhaps it was their tragedy that they could never rise above the status of a colony. Because their titles rested on confiscation they always had to draw assurance from the connection with England, and they could not afford to risk any attempt at bridging the gap between themselves and the papists. While they appealed to 'the glorious revolution' of 1688, many of the things they stood for were precisely what the Whig creed rejected, absolutism, conservatism, sectarianism. It dawned only slowly on Jonathan Swift: 'I ought to let you know' he wrote in 1722, 'that the thing we call a Whig in England is a creature altogether different from those of the same denomination here'.[3] In English eyes they were colonists to be exploited, and English control of the executive ensured that patronage would go to Englishmen, especially in the Church, where there were no undertakers to be placated. Even the protest of 1782 was doomed to futility, for the threatened colony found itself with no real alternative to mother England. The American colonists went on to develop their independence, but the Irish opted for the Union.

They could not even trust the English to share their view of the papists, as was clearly instanced by Chesterfield, lord lieutenant in 1745. The only dangerous papist he knew, he declared, was the beautiful Miss Ambrose, among a 'poor people used worse than negroes by their lords and masters and their deputies of deputies of deputies'. Not that Chesterfield had any love for popery: in fact his plan was to eradicate it by making laws that were relatively mild but enforcing them strictly. He would allow papists to buy and hold property, but he would have all papist property and not just landed property subject to the gavel act. He would legalise Catholic worship but register and control all the Catholic clergy. If the Irish legal system had taken on this shape there would certainly have been a great increase in the number of conformists, and this was precisely what the Irish ascendancy could not afford to contemplate.

Milder popery laws, then, might dilute the settlement by encouraging conversions. But there was more to it than that: the law could not in any way countenance popery because popery could not countenance the law. 'Popery in the gross' was much more than a religion: 'it is destructive both to civil and religious liberty; and under the mask of religion, countenances and sanctifies the most horrid immoralities ... no promises, declarations, or oaths of a popish prince to his Protestant subjects, are ever to be relied on',[4] to quote another of the episcopal charges of 1745. At the beginning of the eighteenth century Catholics not merely gave an allegiance to the pope incompatible with loyalty to the king, but they also recognised as their king a pretender recognised by the pope who had the added disadvantage of being popish himself.

They had some sympathy in their refusal to take the oath of abjuration proposed in the reign of Anne, for, as has been seen, this was couched in terms some Protestants would have found objectionable. There were greater problems in devising a formula by which Catholics could express allegiance to the *de facto* monarchy (how many of them would have been held back by positive support for the Stuarts is not easy to ascertain, but one might reasonably suspect that even among the Catholic bishops not all would have felt impelled to a support in conscience, despite the fact that the pretender had nominated them to their sees). An attempt by some Catholic gentry to find a formula at the accession of George II in 1727 proved premature. It drew fire from the Catholic authorities because it declared that they proffered their loyalty 'from a firm belief of its being a religious duty, which no power on earth can dispense with', and from the civil authorities because it did not contain any abjuration of the Stuart claims.

Yet around mid-century there are indications that although there had been no shift in the legal position and although Catholics still lived with the fear that persecution might be reactivated, social relations between

Catholic and Protestant were developing a quality that might almost be called easiness. In Limerick, the Catholic clergy, with rare exceptions, lived in harmony with the local magnates. One can detect the presence of Protestants at the entertainment offered to the archbishop of Cashel on visitation. The *Constitutio Apostolica* or book of guidance for his clergy in moral matters drawn up by Bishop Nicholas Madgett of Kerry about 1760 is particularly informative. It contains much on fast and abstinence, clearly regarded as an important Catholic community obligation, but can take a sensible view of the fare to be eaten by Catholic servants in Protestant houses, or of the fare to be provided by a Catholic innkeeper for a Protestant guest – in both cases, it is true, with more of an eye to the Catholic's livelihood than to the Protestant's edification. The risk to livelihood also seems the motive in agreeing that Catholic servants may attend prayers in Protestant households, but in some other areas of life one gets a sense of a genuine element of ease in relationships. Bishop Madgett notes that while Protestants sometimes show themselves hostile, they often contribute to the building of Catholic churches. Perhaps the most striking evidence for a real social interaction arises from a consideration of the question of funerals. The bishop poses the question: may Catholics attend the funerals of Protestants? His answer is that they may, that it is what he calls 'the custom of the country' that Catholics and Protestants regularly attend one another's funerals. If, as appears to be the case, the burial of the dead was the most deeply-rooted of religious rites, this is surely significant.

After the outbreak of war between England and France in 1756 things moved quickly. A proposal to revive the Banishment and Registration Acts led Archbishop Michael O'Reilly of Armagh with six other bishops and the support of important Catholic gentry to draw up a letter to the Catholic clergy of Ireland asking them to pray for the king and royal family after Mass each Sunday and holyday, and on the first Sunday of every quarter to read a declaration denying the pope's deposing power and certain other 'odious tenets' imputed to Catholics. The clergy were divided, the nuncio in Brussels smelt Gallicanism, but no great thunders fell. In 1759 an association mainly of Catholic merchants presented an address of loyalty to the speaker of the Irish House of Commons. A new reign began in 1760, and in that same year the pope decided to omit the name of 'James III' in the briefs nominating bishops to Irish sees. In 1763 the Seven Years War ended with the Peace of Paris. Among other things, French Canada was ceded to Britain, and with it its Catholic inhabitants, whose legal rights were secured in the peace treaty. In 1766 James III died, and the papacy did not continue to recognise the royal claims of his son.

The Catholic laity continued to seek a formula in which they could express their loyalty, plucking up courage to defy the reservations and in some cases the hostility of their bishops. In 1774 they got approval of a formula for an oath of allegiance from Archbishop Carpenter of Dublin, and with the help of the Protestant earl-bishop of Derry, Frederick Augustus Hervey, it became law in 1774. Unfortunately, the oath as enshrined in the bill had added to it some phrases at least implicitly disrespectful to the pope. Many Catholics were hostile, including many but not all of the bishops. A number of the laity decided to push the argument in their direction by meeting and taking the oath. This they did by assembling in the Music Hall in Fishamble Street on 28 June 1775 and marching in a body to the court of King's Bench. In a few years most Catholics had followed them. Rome huffed and puffed but refrained from condemnation.[5] The Relief Act of 1778 was more a measure of toleration than genuine emancipation, but the fact that it could be availed of only by those who took the oath meant that in a very real sense a corner had been turned. Catholics were now in some sense, however limited, admitted to the political nation; and all the indications were that their participation would be enlarged. The ideas of the Enlightenment were not confined to the earl-bishop of Derry. Catholics, it was fairly widely felt, had proved they could be trusted. They too were becoming enlightened, and 'popery' was receding into the past. The Holy Roman Emperor, Joseph II, was displaying the shape of Catholicism of the future, and doing it with a disregard for the pope's protests in a way that showed that papal thunders, though they might not yet be abandoned, were certainly ineffective.

All this was a very pleasing prospect to the propertied Catholics. But what of the vast mass of the unpropertied, living in poverty and degradation? The degradation was very real. As Arthur Young wrote in 1779:[6]

> The landlord of an Irish estate, inhabited by Roman Catholics, is a sort of despot who yields obedience, in whatever concerns the poor, to no law but that of his will . . . a long series of oppressions, aided by many very ill-judged laws, have brought landlords into a habit of exerting a very lofty superiority, and their vassals into that of almost unlimited submission . . . A landlord in Ireland can scarcely invent an order which a servant, labourer or cotter dares to refuse to execute. Nothing satisfied him but an unlimited submission. Disrespect or anything tending towards sauciness he may punish with his cane or horsewhip with the most perfect security;

a poor man would have his bones broke if he offered to lift his hand in his own defence. Knocking down is spoken of in this country in a manner that makes an Englishman stare.

Poverty, too, was widespread. At least in the more favoured parts of the country the tenant farmer, however small his holding, went hungry only in the worst famine years, but the growing cottier class, especially those who had to rent their potato patches, could never really make ends meet. Even under the most favourable circumstances their pitiful annual account was in debit and they had to struggle through by God knows what makeshifts, for there was no effective provision for the poor. These are the people that prompted Bishop Berkeley's query: 'Whether there be upon earth any Christian or civilised people so beggarly wretched and destitute as the common Irish', though one might suspect that neither he nor Swift based their denunciations of Irish poverty on any detailed study of the poor. By mid-century there was at least the beginning of population-pressure in its most vicious Irish form, overcrowding of people on the more marginal land as more of the richer lands were turned over to the more profitable cattle. These people, in no way an organic part of civil society, had a tradition of violence: as has been seen, every gathering tended to end in a fight, and the violence of the mob was their only protest against the hardships imposed on them, earlier in the century, for example, by attempts to arrest their priests, or at mid-century when food was moved out of their neighbourhood in the famine years of 1741 and 1756. Even in Connacht, where the old social patterns had been least disturbed, attempts to bring in Protestant tenants were met by outbreaks of cattle-houghing. In the remoter parts the civil law was powerless against organised violence, led by rapparees or near-rapparees, who died out only slowly. The papers of the earls of Kenmare, for instance, are full of references to MacCarthys and O'Donoghues, 'idle and proud', who not only show their discontent with the fact that they are now reduced to the position of tenant farmers by making difficulties in regard to paying their rent, but also impose their will on neighbours who have displeased them by burning crops and 'lifting' cattle.[7] It was just when people like these were coming to the end of their days that organised violence appeared in a new context with the Whiteboy movement.

This broke out in the relatively fertile lands of Munster. Essentially, it was a protest of the poor against a further worsening of their economic situation. As far back as the 1660s Irish cattle had been excluded from the English market. Circumstances during the Seven Years War prompted in 1758 a petition for the repeal of the Cattle Acts. Though they were not formally repealed, Irish cattle were allowed into England in 1758, and Irish beef and butter in 1759. The consequent sharp rise in prices meant little to the cottier, for beef and butter did not figure greatly in his diet. What did affect him, however, was the rise in demand for land for grazing. The land traditionally regarded as 'commons' (though it was not such legally) began to be enclosed. Conacre land for potatoes got scarcer, and its rent rose. The last straw was the tithe on the poor man's potatoes. This was exacted only in Munster and the adjoining parts of Leinster, and it can scarcely be by accident that these were the areas of Whiteboy disturbances.[8]

It has been pointed out that there were Protestants as well as Catholics among the Whiteboys, that there were the more comfortably-off among them as well as the poor, and that they attacked Catholics as well as Protestants. All these points are valid, and they were rightly made from a very early date in answer to the charge that the movement was another example of popish treason. It was in fact a purely economic movement, in no way sectarian nor even in any real sense political. Those involved in it were overwhelmingly the poor, and, given the areas where it took place, that meant the Catholic poor, cottiers, small farmers and their sons, tenants in partnership, strong in the mountain foothills, and craftsmen from the towns, weavers especially, who were often part-time agricultural labourers.

The Catholic establishment opposed the Whiteboys. Catholic landowners and strong farmers were the object of Whiteboy attack equally with Protestants: indeed the very first outbreak was on the estate of a Catholic landowner, Lord Cahir. The Catholic bishops opposed them. They had a long-standing tradition of suspicion of combinations and secret societies, and just at this time they were beginning to associate themselves cautiously with moves for civil recognition of Catholics, at least to the extent of ordering prayers for the king. Nevertheless, the Catholic bishop of Ossory's instruction to his clergy, dated 1 November 1764, to be read on three successive Sundays and to be explained in Irish, must surely have been hard to swallow for at least some of his clergy. The Whiteboys, he wrote, 'if they think themselves grieved in any respect, they might be redressed by lawful ways and means. They ought to be amenable to the laws of the nation, and not provoke the government, which is mild beyond expression'.[9] Yet only a small number of priests are known to have fallen foul of the law in connection with the Whiteboy disturbances, and there is no real reason to believe any of them were actively involved.

The priests in question – five or six of them – came from the area in Tipperary where the disturbances had begun. In 1762 they were presented by the grand jury as not being registered, a charge one would have imagined scarcely needing proof, but it seems to have been brought more by way of warning, for no conviction followed. One of these priests, Nicholas Sheehy, parish priest of Clogheen, was singled out for further prosecution, and it is a fair inference that he had displayed in a particular way whatever quality it was that had led to proceedings against the group. A contemporary Catholic account, by John Curry, is in fact an apologia couched in careful language:[10]

> This man was giddy and officious, but not ill-meaning, with something of a quixotish cast of mind towards relieving all those within his district whom he fancied to be injured or oppressed, and setting aside his unavoidable connection with these rioters, several hundred of whom were his parishioners, he was a clergyman of an unimpeached character in all other respects.

The modern phrase would be that he showed social concern, and his fate showed that it was dangerous at this juncture to show social concern too openly. The 'Whiteboy Act' of 1765 had made several Whiteboy activities capital offences. He was immediately charged under this act. Harassment had already driven him into hiding, but he offered to surrender himself on condition that he would be tried in Dublin and not locally. This was agreed, and the trial ended in an acquittal, because the only evidence produced against him came from three obviously bribed and obviously discreditable witnesses. The pursuit continued, however, and in March 1766 he was put on trial in Clonmel on the charge of murdering a man who had given evidence against the Whiteboys at other trials and who had disappeared. The evidence against Nicholas Sheehy came from the same three witnesses, and witnesses who attempted to testify in his defence were intimidated. He was found guilty, and hanged at Clonmel on 14 March 1766. There can be no doubt it was cold-blooded judicial murder. It was commonly believed that his alleged victim had in fact left the country for his own protection, as several others like him did at the time, and afterwards he was alleged to have been seen alive in Newfoundland. The local establishment may have written off Sheehy after his execution, but he established himself as a martyr in the mind of the frustrated poor. In September 1770 *Sleator's Public Gazetteer* reported:[11]

On Thursday the 6th inst. a man was executed at Philipstown [King's Co.] for murder; during the execution the mob (which was very great) were remarkably quiet, but as soon as it was over, they stoned the hangman to death, and the body lay for two or three days under the gallows. This unfortunate creature was the person who hung Sheehy the priest, which is supposed to be the reason of this outrage.

The reporting would appear to be very accurate. It conveys a mood of grim premeditation, with assembly in sufficient force not only to ensure the job was done, but to cause such intimidation that no one dared to remove the body for two or three days.

It was incidents like this Lecky had in mind when he wrote:[12]

Under the long discipline of the penal laws the Irish Catholics learned the lesson which, beyond all others, rulers should dread to teach. They became consummate addicts in the art of conspiracy and disguise. Secrets known to hundreds were preserved inviolable from authority. False intelligence baffled and distracted the pursuer, and the dread of some fierce nocturnal vengeance was often sufficient to quell the cupidity of the prosecutor.

There can be no doubt of the effectiveness of the Whiteboy organisation, though its more obvious features do not in themselves fully explain this effectiveness. It is true that they are the first known instance of an oath-bound organisation, and certainly the first instance of an effective one. It is true also that intimidation was part of their programme, intimidation cruel at times, though perhaps less noticeably so at a time when the civil law was itself cruel. But oath and intimidation could have produced the results they did only if the ground was very receptive, had been made so by what Lecky called 'the long discipline of the penal laws', that had already made the poor among the Irish Catholics into a secret combination against government and establishment.

I think, however, we can probe a little deeper than the analysis given above, using pieces of information, small but significant, that have been preserved mainly in ascendancy sources. (The folklore tradition might very well provide more details, but here I can claim no competence.) Two women figures appear as the leaders of the Whiteboys – Sive Oultagh and Shevane Meskell. Shevane Meskell suggests little to me, except perhaps a strain of Norman blood, but the more important of the two, Sive Oultagh, does prompt some reflections. She is the 'queen' and the 'mother': the Whiteboys see themselves as 'Queen Sive and her children', her 'fairies' as they often call themselves. 'The fairies are composed of all the able young fellows from Clonmel to Mitchelstown',[13] a Co. Tipperary gentleman declared in 1762. This immediately recalls a note frequently made by Archbishop Butler in his parish visitations of the 1750s, but, perhaps significantly, not before 1759: 'no abuses of superstition, fairy men or women'. It prompts a slight doubt of his confident noting that 'religion appears to be on the increase', a doubt too if he or even his clergy had really penetrated all the recesses of the minds of their people.

The allegorical representation of Ireland as a woman is too well known to need comment. So too is the fact that she has a king-companion. In the Munster eighteenth-century *aisling* tradition she is parted from her king, the Stuart in exile. But the whole thing is so highly idealised that one is left wondering if the Stuart pretender is anything more than a convenient symbol to expound the tradition in the concrete historical circumstances. At times he certainly seems to dissolve into the world of fairy and folklore – in *Mac an Cheannaí*, very strikingly, where the allegory derives from the classical romance, translated into Irish long before, of the beautiful maiden changed into a dragon and fated to remain so until she should be awakened by a kiss from the merchant's son from the land of the west.[14]

But Ireland the woman found another line of expression, not as a young maiden but as an old woman, and by the standards not just of tridentine Catholicism but of any conceivable brand of Christianity not a very respectable woman, the *striapach*, the harlot queen, who has had and discarded many kings in her time. This immediately puts one in mind of the ceremony of the inauguration of a king that Christianity found in Ireland in the fifth century and that persisted down to the extinction of the Gaelic lordships. As its centre was the essentially pagan religious ceremony of the wedding of the king to his kingdom. And behind that one can sense even older things, memories of the land as earth-mother, of the mother-goddess. Something like this surely lies behind the ambivalent position of the great queens in that oldest strand of the literary tradition, the *Táin Bó Cuailnge*.

It is time to return to Queen Sive to show that all this may not have left the ground. Sive or Sadb is also a name that hovers on the edges of the underworld, of goddesses and great queens. Moreover, she is associated with the Osraighe people and with the Fionn sagas, that derive from Leinster and the south midlands, the territory between the two nurturing-places of Fionn himself, the Slieve Blooms and the Galtees. This is precisely the countryside of Kilkenny and Tipperary now the centre of Whiteboy disturbances. Here Sive is still in some sense 'queen' and 'mother'. When her subjects call her 'Oultagh' it indicates that she like them has come down in the world, for 'Oultagh' is *Ultach* (Dinneen gives *Olltach* as a Munster variant), and the *cailleach Ultach* is the witch, surely reflecting a folk-tradition spread far wider than Ireland, that the dark powers lived in the north.

We can now slot in a piece of evidence noted in, of all places, *Exshaw's Magazine* for June 1762, a common rallying-cry of the Whiteboys, 'Long live King George III and Queen Sive'. It was not surprising that they should have no special grudge against the king, for it was not he who was oppressing them, but the local squireens of Tipperary. Neither would it have been a complication that they were to come to venerate Father Sheehy as a martyr, for he perished at the hands of the squireens and not of King George. But Father Sheehy might well have been embarrassed had he understood them – and it seems hard to understand them any other way – as meaning that the old *striapach* Queen Sive was now seeking George III as a husband. And yet there was a great realism to it, in comparison with the dying literary conventions of the *aisling*. The Tipperary peasantry were not too far removed from their bishops and gentry in reaching out towards an accommodation with the Hanoverians.

It would clearly be foolish to pretend to any measure of certainty in what has just been said. In explaining the figure of the queen who is also a poor old woman, account should possibly be taken of the strain of goliardic and even black humour that runs through Irish expression, though Donnelly notes that the group where perhaps one might expect this to originate, the schoolmasters, were not really prominent until the 1790s and that little is heard of them among the earliest Whiteboys.[15] However, while we may still be far from the answers, it may be that we are on the road to the right questions.

If so, there is another reason to suspect that we should not expect to find anything that could be described as revolutionary in this first outbreak of peasant Ireland, and so it proves. What they sought was reform. Their first protest was against the landlords' enclosure of 'commons' that had pushed up the rent of the poor man's potato-patch. From this there developed a protest against the burden of rents, but again seeking reform, not abolition. Their principal target was the practice of 'canting', whereby the land was regularly put up to the highest bidder without regard to the tenant in possession. The protest then spread to the tithe, because in the Whiteboy areas the tithe bore especially heavily on the potatoes of the poor, and possibly, as has been suggested, because the parson was less protected than the landlord. Here again, however, they seek reform and not abolition. They will pay a fair tithe. Their principal objection is not to the tithe-proctor, who collects the tithe, if he collects it for the parson, but to the tithe-farmer, who makes his profit by screwing what he can out of them. Neither do they object to the tithe-canter, who buys the right to collect small portions of tithe, because many poor people are tithe-canters in a modest way. They give a little money to the parson for the right to collect a little food from what was due in tithe.

The overall discipline of the Whiteboys was quite remarkable, in a society where violence could break out so easily and spontaneously, indicating that this protest against widespread oppression was a little more complex than a straightforward *jacquerie*. Yet the edge of revolution was not there. Neither was the edge of sectarianism. Perhaps too much could be made of the fact that some Protestants were involved (they were involved twenty years later, but in different circumstances), but the general attitude of the Whiteboys towards rent and tithe indicates no sectarian aim. It would be interesting, though in the present state of our knowledge probably difficult, to trace the process by which the word 'Sasanach' came in familiar speech to have the meaning of 'Protestant', especially in Munster. A proclamation of 13 September 1765 recites that 'a great concourse of lawless rioters assembled at Rossconnell in the County of Kilkenny ... under appearance of religious ceremonies, at a place commonly called a patron', where they assaulted several gentlemen, 'crying down with the Sassanahs, meaning the Protestants'.[16] This was Whiteboy country, and one must have lingering doubts about the accuracy of the gloss, if it may not be more accurate to see the gentry hated not because they were Protestants but because they were despoilers and oppressors: as it was put to one of them in a Whiteboy letter:[17]

> She [Sive Oultagh] and her company does not intend or mean following any bad practice, but to the contrary, to relieve the poor who are oppressed by most people and especially by tithe-mongers, whom she intends obstructing in their exorbitant prices, and also to open commonages, and level them.

The reaction of the establishment was calculated to introduce a sectarian element if at all possible. Spontaneously, they applied for troops, and in default of troops they armed their Protestant tenants and retainers. Spontaneously too they raised the cry of a 'popish rebellion' with French backing, and spoke fearsomely of the planned massacre of Protestants. They could not really have feared 'popery' as a religion, if only because the Catholic Church authorities condemned the Whiteboys, nor could they have really feared a Jacobite connection. What they feared was the old bugbear of 'popery in the gross', above all its threat to the land settlement. The response of the Irish administration was markedly different. Here there appears very clearly the divergence of attitude and interest as between the Irish ascendancy and the English-born members of the administration. A special commission to deal with the Whiteboy disturbances was set up under Richard Aston, chief justice of the Common Pleas. Born in England, Aston had been appointed to this high post in the Irish judiciary in 1761. His verdict was that the causes of the trouble were economic, that they were in no way sectarian, and that there was not 'the least reason to impute these disturbances to disaffection to his majesty, his government, or the laws in general'. He imposed very few capital sentences, and there were many acquittals. At Clonmel one man was sentenced to a year in prison, and all the rest were acquitted. When he left the town the road was lined with people who knelt for his blessing. He had not endeared himself to the gentry and he resigned his Irish post in 1765. The lord lieutenant, the earl of Halifax, was of the same mind. He reported that the disturbances were caused by poverty, that they were in no sense sectarian, and that the way to end them was for the propertied classes to exercise 'justice and lenity'.

The 'Whiteboy Act' of 1765 made many of the actions of the Whiteboys capital offences, and allowed the grand juries to levy compensation on baronies where outrages had taken place. Nevertheless, the repression of the Whiteboys cannot be considered severe overall: there was a total of twenty-six death sentences. It was hard to get people to initiate a process, or even to give evidence, and even after 1765 juries were unwilling to find prisoners guilty of capital charges. There can be no doubt that there was still a real fear of Whiteboy vengeance. The movement petered out in the second half of the decade, not so much because it had been defeated by the forces of the law, but because of the very severe economic conditions that set in after the bad harvest of 1765. There had been no attempt to deal with the economic pressures that had caused it, and the prospect of further outbreaks remained. They came in Kilkenny, where the Whiteboys were least cowed. The opposition of the Catholic leaders not only on the religious but also at the social level was apparent at Ballyraggett in February 1775, when a small group of Catholics, led by the parish priest, and organised by Archbishop James Butler of Cashel, defended against a Whiteboy attack the house of the local landlord, Robert Butler, the archbishop's brother. A little more than twelve months later, in March 1776, the papers were reporting an attack on Eugene Geoghegan, the coadjutor Catholic bishop of Meath. He had forcefully denounced the Whiteboys, and that they were his assailants was known from the fact that he had fired at them down the stairs and killed a man who proved to be a well-known Whiteboy leader. But despite these evidences of strain in the Catholic community it could still be claimed that it was a popish rebellion led by the priests. In November 1775 Ambrose Power was murdered. A landlord and magistrate, he had taken an active part in the events that had led to Father Sheehy's execution. Once again there was blood for blood, with two men executed for the murder in Clonmel in January 1776, cut down alive, quartered and beheaded, while the gentlemen of the county looked on, heavily armed and protected by troops. Other executions followed, and a new Crimes Act was passed to strengthen the legislation of 1765.

The 1770s too had seen a marked development of trade unionism in Dublin. The workers who were trying to organise themselves were not the poor, but skilled workers, 'journeymen', still regulated by a medieval guild system where, however, they had lost all power to the master-craftsmen. The response of the journeymen was unionisation, and as this was opposed by the masters it led to violence and rioting, not the mindless violence more or less endemic in the poorer parts of the city, but violence organised with a purpose, especially where there was question of 'scab' labour. It may be presumed that the journeyman workforce was mostly Protestant, but that there must have been a fair number of Catholics among them is clear from a series of admonitions from Archbishop Carpenter.[18] Trade unions he disapproved of in themselves – 'such combinations are unchristian and unlawful' – but it is also clear that he feared that the activities of Catholic workmen might be used as an excuse to delay concessions to Catholics. The first concessions did come precisely in these years, and they were so reluctantly doled out that one can see why he was afraid.

There had been stirrings too in rural Ulster, always a danger spot, for here Catholics and Protestants competed on the same economic level, and economic grievances could easily become sectarian. In spite of the widespread cottage industry, it was not a rich province. In the opinion of Arthur Young, who on this point may be assumed to have known what he was talking about, the fact that so many could earn money by weaving had led to a great fragmentation of holdings, worse than indifferently farmed: 'behold a whole province peopled by weavers; it is they who cultivate, or rather beggar the soil, as well as work the looms; agriculture is there in ruins ... no other part of Ireland can exhibit the soil in such a state of poverty and desolation'.[19] Ulster's lasting problem was already threatening: in a poor community, more for poor Catholics meant less for poor Protestants.

The first disturbances, those of the Oakboys in 1763, were put down fairly easily. The Steelboys of 1771 were, however, a more serious threat, though practically confined to the vast estates of the marquis of Donegal. He decided to raise his rents and charge high entry-fines when leases fell in, as a number of them did just at this time. There may have been some economic justification for his action, but some of his tenants were not able to meet the increased charges and were turned out. Some farms went to Catholics, and this raised the sectarian issue. A Steelboy petition to the viceroy in 1772 declared:[20]

> That we are all Protestants and Protestant Dissenters, and bear unfeigned loyalty to his present majesty and the Hanoverian succession
> . . .
> That some of us by refusing to pay the extravagant rent demanded by our landlords have been turned out, and our lands given to papists, who will pay any rent.

This is a claim to be part of 'the Protestant interest'. The claim was not accepted. The reaction of the establishment was the same as it had been to the Whiteboys in the Catholic south. The viceroy, Viscount Townsend, said what his predecessor had said of the Munster disturbances, that the problem was economic and that justice would solve it. Those who could solve it, through their representatives in parliament, reacted with repressive measures. These helped to quiet the situation in Ulster, but even more important was a massive increase in the numbers of Presbyterian emigrants to America, where they would shortly have their revenge in the war of independence. Behind them in Ulster they left the shadow of sectarian conflict between the Catholic and Protestant poor.

This conflict worsened with the rise of the Peep of Day boys. After 1783 the Volunteers began to break up. Only the more radical groups attempted to keep going, and they welcomed more Catholics into their ranks, though Catholics could not legally carry arms. This prospect alarmed Protestant Ulster. Its response was the Peep of Day boys, so called from their early morning raids for arms on Catholic houses. The Catholics responded by organising themselves as Defenders. The level of outrage and violence was higher than anything previously known, and the issues were now clearly sectarian, with the wrecking of Catholic chapels and a concerted attempt to drive Catholics out of Ulster, especially out of Co. Armagh.

In 1778 the first real steps were taken towards a repeal of the penal laws. They were taken under some pressure from England, and contrasted unfavourably with the concessions given to English Catholics that same year. Existing Catholic estates were protected by the repeal of the gavel act and those acts favouring a son who conformed to the Established Church, but Catholics were still forbidden to acquire new landed property by freehold, though parliament was almost evenly divided on an issue that was far more emotional than economic, for the measure actually carried allowed Catholics to take land for 999 years at a money rent. This rent was not specified, and might be purely nominal, as indeed it seems to have been expected it would be. However, 'leasehold' had not the political overtones of the emotive even if ill-defined word 'freehold', the tenure worthy of a free man. Strong elements of the grudging spirit remain in the Relief Act of 1782, though many Protestants did in fact believe that Catholics should be generously treated. These sentiments emerged at the Dungannon convention of the Volunteers in February and in a number of speeches in parliament, notably those of Henry Grattan, who put the issue bluntly: it was a choice between remaining a Protestant settlement or becoming an Irish nation. Parliament's answer was at best hesitant. They swallowed – or more accurately, nearly swallowed – the bitter medicine of the land problem, allowing Catholics to buy and bequeath land like Protestants, but provided it was not situated in a parliamentary borough. Hesitations are very evident in matters of religion. A number of laws affecting the clergy that had long fallen into disuse were repealed, but the act of repeal reaffirmed others that marked off papists as inferior – provisions against converts to popery, against mixed marriages, against Catholics assuming ecclesiastical titles or rank, against priests officiating outside their accustomed places of worship or wearing vestments outside the chapel, which must not have a bell or steeple. Education was allowed, under licence from the Protestant bishop, but there could be no popish university or college or endowed school.

Meanwhile, economic discontent simmered on. A new outbreak of violence took place in 1785 on the borders of Cork and Kerry. Its perpetrators called themselves the 'Rightboys', and this name seems well on the way to being adopted for the disturbances which followed, though contemporaries, by and large, continued to use the term 'Whiteboy'. The events of the 1780s have a great deal in common with those of the 1760s and 1770s, but there are sufficient differences between them to make it at least convenient to distinguish them by a different name.

Donnelly[21] lists the similarities – both movements are 'regional', that is, more than local, less than national; in both cases the grievances are economic, not sectarian; both use very much the same tactics; and both seek essentially reform, not revolution. In some respects, however, the Rightboy movement was far more formidable. It spread more widely and it attracted more widespread support from different social classes. The reasons for this were again economic. The economic changes about 1760 had borne most heavily on the potato patches of the poor. In 1784 Foster's Corn Law had increased the profitability of Irish grain. Land for grain growing was in greatly increased demand and in consequence more expensive. As grasslands were broken up for tillage they became subject to the tithe, which now became a grievance of the better off in the same way as the tithe of potatoes had earlier been a grievance of the poor. Attack on the tithe was now coming on a very broad front. Again, the demand was not for abolition, but for reform, though as the Rightboy movement rapidly gained confidence there was a rising demand that reforms should extend to the abolition of the most hated exactions, such as the tithe on potatoes, county cess, church rates and hearth-money.

By the spring of 1786 the movement had certainly gained confidence. Public marches by great numbers took place in the daylight hours. The Rightboys were using the assembly of the people for Sunday Mass to tender their oaths to the community as a whole. At this time too the attack was mounted on the dues and services payable to the Catholic clergy. These demands were firmly made and accompanied with menaces – particularly recalcitrant priests had their chapels attacked, and sometimes their persons. They were moderate, however, in the sense that there was a clear recognition that the Catholic clergy did not dispose of the wealth of the Established Church, though by this date it was clear that many of them were indeed comfortably off, that they led a distinctly 'middle class' existence that is already apparent in the Cashel visitations of the 1750s. A rising population had brought more fees from christenings, marriages and funerals, and these were also occasions for the entertainment of the clergy. The development of 'stations of confession' in a number of houses through the parish had further multiplied the occasions on which the priest was due a fee and expected entertainment, further increasing his revenue and cutting his expenses. His living standard was now high enough to cause real resentment, shown most strikingly by the numbers who refused his services, some of them even making what seems to have been in most cases a brief stay in the Established Church. How real the resentment was emerges too from the real concern shown by the Catholic bishops.[22] While they denounced the Rightboys as severely as they had earlier denounced the Whiteboys, and for the same reasons, they were clearly worried that some priests by their exactions had given real cause for the grievances.

The Rightboys developed into a formidable movement as increased support came from the better-off. The poor naturally provided the ranks of the marchers, and they continued to provide most of the leaders. But leadership was also coming from the better-off farmers and even the landed gentry, though most of these latter were not prepared to go beyond passive support for non-violent action. The motives of those prepared to commit themselves actively were in most cases self-interested, though with a small number there is evidence of a real social concern. The fact was that very few were prepared to defend the tithe-system, and it did begin to appear as if this common interest might generate a real social revolution. At least the smell of it was in the air.

It is hard to be certain of the level of violence. The apparatus for law-enforcement and the notification of crime was still rudimentary, and its records have survived only in fragments. Fear tended to attribute all crimes to the Rightboys, and to insist that they were motivated by a wish to overthrow the government, but examples have survived of Rightboy disclaimers of individual outrages attributed to them and of the general charge of disaffection to the crown. By the standards of agrarian outrages of the nineteenth century it appears clear that the level of violence was low. Donnelly makes what seems a telling comment when he notes that 'what greatly surprised upper-class contemporaries about the disturbances was that so little serious violence took place',[23] and this seems true both in regard to violence against property and against the person. It has been already noted that some Catholic priests suffered violence. The ministers of the Established Church might be expected to suffer more, because the grievances against them were greater. There do seem to be instances of serious personal violence offered to them, but it also seems clear that such assaults were exceptional. One reason why they were exceptional is because they were unnecessary. In most instances intimidation was quite sufficient to bring about the lowering of tithes the Rightboys demanded. It would appear that only five murders can be clearly attributed to them, and of these three were not premeditated.

The Whiteboy Act of 1787 added to the long list of capital offences introduced in 1765, but its main concern was to secure a more effective enforcement of the law, and the beginning of a recognition that in Ireland the English model for local justice would not be enough. The Act proposed the appointment of stipendiary magistrates, and the setting up of a barony constabulary, who, though appointed by the grand juries, in effect the leading local gentry, were to be under the control of peace-officers nominated by the crown. These measures could not be expected to bring an immediate improvement, and though concerted attempts were made to bring Rightboys to trial, convictions were few and sentences generally light. The reasons seem clear. The overall level of serious violence had in fact been low. The Rightboys had relied rather on a very real capacity for intimidation, and this now worked to dissuade people from initiating procedures or from giving evidence, and making jurors unwilling to find prisoners guilty of charges carrying heavy penalties. It is true that violence died down quite quickly, but this was probably due less to the effectiveness of the legal processes than to a growing conviction that there would soon be a reform of grievances, especially of the tithe.

The Irish tithe-system had few friends and many enemies. A fundamental inequity arose from the fact that the Established Church was a minority, over much of Ireland a small minority. This inequity was compounded by the fact that the tithe bore hardest on the poor, most of them not members of the Established Church. The gentry were now less inclined to support the system, for a variety of reasons, ranging from the spread of Enlightenment ideas to the switch from grass to corn. The tithe was a long-standing grievance with the Presbyterians: it had been high on the list of Oakboy complaints in the 1760s. The grievance against the tithe inclined to broaden into the demand for general reform: specifically, the question was raised whether there should be a church establishment at all. The Presbyterians were very vocally opposed to it, and some of their more radical members, especially in Belfast, were well disposed to Catholics. The phrases were taking shape: 'the common name of Irishman' and even 'the men of no property'. Catholic and Presbyterian had found coinciding enmities that might well develop into common interests.

In parliament, Grattan was giving special attention to the tithe. He had supported the repressive legislation of 1787, while insisting that there must also be reform of the abuses that had led to violence, of the tithe-system in particular. In 1787, 1788 and 1789 he introduced bills to this end. They aimed at making the tithe a less arbitrary charge, to make it easier to pay and in consequence easier to collect. These changes would not have notably diminished the revenue of the Established Church. Yet Grattan's proposals met head-on resistance from the bishops, on the grounds that they were an attack on ancient rights. With greater blindness they argued against a change in the system on conscientious, one might almost say theological, grounds, that it would be the beginning of the ruin of the establishment. Grattan's measures were doomed when he failed to get the support of the administration, and the tide had turned against any reform. His third bill was lost in 1789, the last year of the old regime in Europe.

There can be no doubt that the 1790s were, in Ireland as elsewhere, a crucial decade, a real turning point. Many frustrations boiled over, and many issues came to a head. So much happened so rapidly that it is not easy to tread surely through these years. Among the Protestant poor there was a great sensitivity to any rise in the status of Catholics. With the Protestant ascendancy there was a particular sensitivity to their getting a political voice. The failure of one reform measure after another meant that the reformers became more radical. The United Irishmen, founded in November 1791, represented essentially the urban radical protest of Dublin and Belfast. The Catholic political leaders were going in the same direction. In the months immediately following the foundation of the United Irishmen, in December 1791 and January 1792, the aristocracy and gentry seceded from the Catholic Committee, and leadership passed to the Dublin merchants with John Keogh at their head. In January a Catholic Relief Bill had passed with little opposition. It had made wide concessions, but had specifically rejected any move towards admission of Catholics to the political processes by way of the parliamentary vote or the holding of office under the crown. A mildly-worded Catholic petition arguing that Catholics might now be trusted in the body politic was scornfully rejected. One 'patriot' member described it as emanating from 'the rabble of the town'. French parallels suggest themselves: this might well be the Irish equivalent of 'let them eat cake'.

In July 1792 Theobald Wolfe Tone, one of the founders of the United Irishmen, became full-time secretary of the Catholic Committee. Using his organising abilities, Keogh arranged elections for a Catholic Convention. The name was ominous. The French had imprisoned King Louis XVI in August, as the experiment of a constitutional monarchy collapsed. The National Convention met in Paris in September 1792, with the country at war with the European monarchies. The Irish Catholic Convention met in Dublin in December, in the Tailors' Hall in Back Lane. It decided to petition the king directly, bypassing parliament and the lord lieutenant. This resulted in the Relief Act of 1793, which gave Catholics the political rights denied them the previous year and also the right to bear arms. The militia raised immediately afterwards was largely Catholic. These concessions had come because of fear of the power of the organised Catholics, but even more because of pressure from Pitt, the British prime minister, who had reluctantly decided that it would have to be war against revolutionary France, and was not prepared to face the prospect of an alliance between Catholics and radicals in Ireland.

Though they could not yet take a seat in parliament because of the oaths required, the Catholic middle classes were content with their achievement. Down in Derrynane, Maurice 'Hunting Cap' O'Connell entered the new age by becoming a justice of the peace. A few years later, with a French fleet in Bantry Bay, his nephew Daniel was to note in his diary: 'the Irish are not yet sufficiently enlightened to bear the sun of freedom. Freedom would soon degenerate into licentiousness. They would rob, they would plunder ...'.[24] No political figure really understood the grievances of the poor. Tone did not grasp them and neither did Grattan. In so far as it is possible to understand their problems, they had little to do with parliamentary reform or with the rights of man. When they spoke of 'liberty' what they had in mind was delivery from tithes and taxes and a relaxation of the burden of rent that would give them a little better grip on the land. There are scant indications that they felt their lot would be bettered by throwing off allegiance to the throne, and sufficient indications that they had no real desire to do so. When, therefore, the United Irishmen were suppressed in 1794 and reorganised themselves as an underground movement, increasingly revolutionary and republican, while it was very natural that they should try to establish contact with peasant radicalism there were in fact few points of real contact. The Defenders spread through Catholic Ireland, but though they spoke a language of revolution that might seem to have much in common with the United Irishman, even with the Defender leaders the resemblance was only superficial, and with the rank and file it must have been very superficial indeed. The cause of the Defenders was essentially the old social radicalism of the Whiteboys, a cause, incidentally, that would have received scant sympathy from the United Irish leaders, including Wolfe Tone himself.[25]

In Ulster, the Catholic Defenders fought the Protestants in a sectarian peasant war.[26] Sectarianism worsened with the foundation of the Orange Order after the 'battle of the Diamond' in September 1795. There had always been an 'Orange tradition', cherishing the memory of William III, who had brought delivery from 'popery, slavery, arbitrary power, brass money and wooden shoes'. It continued through the eighteenth century, but with the propertied classes under the influence of the Enlightenment and especially of freemasonry it inclined to take a liberal attitude to Catholics or at least to be critical of the penal code. It had little in common with the movement newly founded in Ulster. It was natural that the first reaction of the ascendancy to this should be one of suspicion. Since the days of the Oakboys they had made it clear that they shared no common interest with the Protestant peasantry. Yet the pressures of the times brought them together. When in 1796 it was decided to establish yeomanry corps it had been planned to enrol Catholics as well as Protestants, but in practice the yeomanry became exclusively Protestant. On 4 June 1797 a group of Protestant gentry in Dublin formed themselves into an Orange lodge. By the spring of 1798 the lord lieutenant, the earl of Camden, 'the very type of the British aristocrat ... young and tall and fair-haired ... high-minded and humane',[27] was fighting a losing battle with the Irish junta, three elderly men, John Beresford, John Foster, and John Fitzgibbon, earl of Clare. What they were urging was the 'Protestant policy' they had reluctantly abandoned in 1793, a policy that now involved an alliance between the ascendancy and the Orangemen.

Under pressure, Camden yielded. On 10 March 1798 he agreed to the arrest of the leaders of the United Irishmen. This meant that if, and as events were shortly to show, when an insurrection came in the Catholic south it would not be the insurrection the United Irishmen had planned. Though the insurgents might plant 'trees of liberty' their aims were not so much revolutionary or republican as the redress of social and ancient wrongs. Neither was it to be a religious war, except in a qualified sense. It necessarily took on a religious aspect because the insurgents were Catholics and those they regarded as their oppressors were Protestants. Here history may be teetering on the brink of moral judgements perhaps better avoided, but it is hard to avoid returning to the thought that the decisive turning-point came when the privileged classes deliberately exploited in their own interests the sectarian elements in the basically economic antagonisms of the poor. The legacy was bitter. Among the Catholics there was certainly an explicit sectarianism in the nineteenth century that had been unknown in the eighteenth.

The insurrection was not the one the United Irishmen had planned: indeed it had not been planned at all. In consequence, the insurgents had to find their own leaders. It has already been noted that in Wexford they can be seen to fall into three groups, each having a natural respect in the community. Firstly there was the minority of 'liberal' landlords (one reason why Wexford was an area of particular tension seems to have been because there the local gentry were particularly polarised in their political views). Secondly, there were the Catholic clergy. Here too there were divisions. They provided many of the leaders, but numbers of them were opposed to the rising, Bishop Caulfield, for example, and perhaps particularly the town clergy. Thirdly there were the substantial Catholic farmers, still respected because they were regarded as the descendants of former proprietors.

A thoughtful book by Barbara Solow argues that after the Famine the Irish landlord system had in fact made for substantial economic progress, but that the tenant farmer sought land-purchase not just because he believed it had not, but also because he was convinced that ownership of his land was the only thing that could give him real independence and dignity. Another historian of the Irish land-question in the nineteenth century, E. D. Steele,[28] maintains that in Ireland 'tenant-right' meant more than it did in England, where it was understood as simply compensation for outlays or improvements. In Ireland, on the other hand, it was understood as a saleable asset of the tenant, implying that he had a real and independent interest in the land. Mrs Solow ends her book with some reflections on the reactions of James Martin of Ross in Connemara to the fact that in the election of 1872 his tenants for the first time voted against his wishes.[29] The Martins had been one of the great merchant families of Galway. In 1590 they had begun buying land in Connemara, and over the seventeenth century bought up most of the former O'Flaherty estates. They showed great capacity for survival. In 1698 'Nimble Dick' Martin obtained terms from William III that made him virtually king in Connemara. But by mid-century the pressures of the penal code had caught up with his son, Robert. Robert had been one of the few active Jacobites in Ireland during the forty-five. Shortly afterwards he conformed to the Established Church, quite simply to save the estate, but his change of religion brought no change in the patriarchal relation between him and his tenants.

Violet Florence Martin is much better known by her pen-name, 'Martin Ross'. In 1872 she was ten years old, the youngest daughter of the house. In her memoirs, written in 1906, she recalled her father's reaction to the election. It was not the political defeat that wounded him most. The fact that his tenants had not obeyed his wishes was the real wound, a betrayal of personal trust. 'Martin Ross' recalled too how on a visit home in 1880 she met an old family retainer, 'whom Carlie and I used to beat with sticks 'til he was "near dead", as he himself says proudly'. Mrs Solow comments: 'Eventually, one supposes, he stopped being proud of being beaten with sticks'. It prompts a thought that when a man like Edward Roche of Garrylough in Co. Wexford decided in 1798 to assert his rights in the political nation by becoming an insurgent it may have been just because he had got tired of being called 'Roche'. His political views would have had much more of Grattan than of Tone to them, and it may well be asked if the political views of the 'Croppy Boy' who accepted his leadership had very much of either of them.

Notes

What follows might be described as a combination of bibliography and footnotes. I have kept detailed annotation to a minimum, normally using it only for direct quotations. Much of the material used is either unprocessed or has been only partially processed. I have felt it most useful to indicate source-material or further reading at selected points in the text.

The following bibliographical abbreviations have been used in addition to those listed in *Irish Historical Studies:*

Brady, *Eighteenth-century press*
> J. Brady, *Catholics and catholicism in the eighteenth-century press* (Maynooth, 1965).

Burke, *Penal times*
> W. P. Burke, *The Irish priests in the Penal times 1660–1760* (Waterford, 1914, reprinted Shannon, 1969).

Carrigan, *Ossory*
> W. Carrigan, *The history and antiquities of the diocese of Ossory* (4 vols., Dublin, 1905).

Cogan, *Meath*
> A. Cogan, *The ecclesiastical history of the diocese of Meath* (3 vols., Dublin, 1867–74)

Comerford, *Kildare and Leighlin*
> D. Comerford, *Collections relating to the dioceses of Kildare and Leighlin* (3 vols., Dublin, 1883–6).

Father Luke Wadding
> *Father Luke Wadding: commemorative volume,* edited by the Franciscan Fathers, Dún Mhuire, Killiney (Dublin, 1957).

Hore, *Wexford*
> P. H. Hore, *History of the town and county of Wexford* (6 vols., London, 1900–11).

Jn. Ecc. Hist.
> *Journal of Ecclesiastical History* (Cambridge, 1950 ff.).

Measgra Mhichíl Uí Chléirigh
> S. O'Brien (ed.), *Measgra i gchuimhne Mhichíl Uí Chléirigh* (Dublin, 1944).

N.H.I.
> T. W. Moody, F. X. Martin and F. J. Byrne (eds.), *A New History of Ireland,* iii (Oxford, 1976).

Renehan, *Collections*
> L. F. Renehan, *Collections on Irish Church History* (ed. D. McCarthy, 2 vols., Dublin, 1861, 1874).

Studies in Ir. hist. presented to R. Dudley Edwards
> A. Cosgrove and D. McCartney (eds.), *Studies in Irish history presented to R. Dudley Edwards* (Dublin, 1979).

Chapter I (pp 1–17)
1. In *Hist. Studies*, viii, 155–69.
2. Letter of Gregory to Mellitus in Bede, *Hist. ecc.* (ed. C. Plummer, Oxford, 1896), i, 65.
3. Quoted by Robin Flower, *The Irish Tradition* (Oxford, 1947) pp 30–31, from W. Stokes (ed.), *The Martyrology of Oengus* (London, 1905), p. 154.
4. A. Cosgrove, 'Hiberniores ipsis Hibernis' in *Studies in Ir. hist. presented to R. Dudley Edwards*, pp 1–14.
5. 'Ecclesiastical appointments in the province of Tuam, 1399–1477' in *Archiv. Hib.*, xxxiii (1975), pp 91–100.
6. C. Mooney, *The Church in Gaelic Ireland: thirteenth to fifteenth centuries* (Dublin, 1969); K. Nicholls, *Gaelic and Gaelicised Ireland in the Middle Ages* (Dublin, 1972), pp 91–113.
7. For the monks and friars see especially B. Bradshaw, *The Dissolution of the Religious Orders in Ireland under Henry VIII* (Cambridge, 1974), pp 8–38.
8. *S. P. Hen. VIII*, ii, 570.
9. See the chapter on the religious drama in St. John D. Seymour, *Anglo-Irish Literature, 1200–1582* (Cambridge, 1929), pp 118–34.
10. Mooney, op. cit., especially pp 18–20, 32–52.
11. Nicholls, op. cit., pp 73, 91.
12. *A History of Medieval Ireland* (Dublin, 1927), p. 426.
13. N. Canny, *The Formation of the Old English Elite in Ireland* (Dublin, 1975); B. Bradshaw, *The Irish Constitutional Revolution of the Sixteenth Century* (Cambridge, 1979), pp 32–57.
14. *S. P. Hen. VIII*, ii, 1–31.
15. B. Bradshaw, 'Manus "the Magnificent": O'Donnell as a Renaissance Prince' in *Studies in Ir. Hist. presented to R. Dudley Edwards*, pp 15–37.
16. *S. P. Hen. VIII*, iii, 320. No doubt O'Donnell had his own good reasons for suggesting that Elphin was in the 'province of Thomond'.
17. C. Mhág Craith, *Dán na mbráthar mionúr* (Dublin, 1967), p. 375:
    Poor friar overcome with wine!
    Wake him not, though waked he should be;
    Step by him gently, quietly;
    Let Aodh have a snore for himself for a while.
18. Mooney, op. cit., pp 41–2; Flower, op. cit., pp 133–5:
    Fairer is Jesus than earth's orb,
    Than bloom of rose or lily;
    Beloved flower sprung from Mary,
    You have entered into lasting kinship bond with us.
19. J. Bossy, 'The Counter-reformation and the people of Catholic Europe' in *Past & Present*, no. 47 (May, 1970), pp 51–70, is an excellent summary of the conclusions of the French 'sociological' historians.
20. B. Bradshaw, 'Sword, word and strategy in the Reformation in Ireland' in *Hist. Jn.*, xxi (1978), pp 475–502; N. Canny, 'Why the Reformation failed in Ireland: *une question mal posée*' in *Jn. Ecc. Hist.*, xxx (1979), pp 1–28.

Chapter 2 (pp 18–42)
Attention has already been called to John Bossy, 'The Counter-reformation and the people of Catholic Ireland' in *Hist. Studies*, viii, 153–70. With it might be listed H. F.

Kearney, 'Ecclesiastical politics and the Counter-reformation in Ireland' in *Jn. Ecc. Hist.*, xi (1960), pp 202–12; A. Clarke, 'Colonial identity in early seventeenth-century Ireland' in T. W. Moody (ed.), *Nationality and the pursuit of National Independence* (Belfast, 1978), pp 57–72; P. J. Corish, 'The reorganisation of the Irish Church, 1603–41' in *Ir. Cath. Hist. Comm. Proc.* (1957), pp 9–14.

1. For the situation in England, with some reference to Holland, see, with certain reservations, P. Hughes, *Rome and the Counter-reformation in England* (London, 1944), pp 271–430.

2. As, for example, in W. M. Brady, *The Episcopal Succession in England, Scotland and Ireland* (Rome, 1876) or F. M. Jones, 'Canonical faculties on the Irish mission in the reign of Queen Elizabeth' in *Ir. Theol. Quart.*, xx (1953), pp 152–71.

3. See J. J. Silke, 'Primate Peter Lombard and Hugh O'Neill' in *Ir. Theol. Quart.*, xxii (1955), pp 15–30; 'Primate Lombard and James II', ibid., pp 124–49.

4. P. J. Corish, 'An Irish Counter-reformation bishop: John Roche' in *Ir. Theol Quart.*, xxvi (1959), p. 107; Clarke, art. cit., p. 65.

5. There is much human detail in D. Cregan, 'The social and cultural background of a Counter-reformation episcopate' in *Studies in Ir. hist. presented to R. Dudley Edwards*, pp 85–117.

6. Much of our detailed information on the functions of *coarbs* and *erenaghs* comes from the Ulster inquisitions and Davies, *Discovery*. See also in particular Gwynn, *Med. province Armagh*.

7. This breakdown is given by D. Buckley, 'Diocesan organisation: Cloyne' in *Ir. Cath. Hist. Comm. Proc.* (1956), pp 8–11.

8. Much information on the condition of the Established Church is to be found in the royal visitations. For a guide see P. B. Phair, 'Seventeenth-century regal visitations' in *Anal. Hib.*, xxviii (1978), pp 79–102, with indications of the published visitations, principally in *Archiv. Hib.*, i–iv, viii. See also C. V. Jourdan in *Ch. of Ire.*, ii, 376–579. On the insecurities of the Established Church see the interesting paper by P. Kilroy, 'Sermon and pamphlet literature in the Irish reformed Church, 1613–34' in *Archiv. Hib.*, xxxiii (1975), pp 110–21.

9. B. Bradshaw, 'Sword, word and strategy in the Reformation in Ireland' in *Hist. Jn.*, xxi (1978), pp 475–502; N. Canny, 'Why the Reformation failed in Ireland: *une question mal posée*' in *Jn. Ecc. Hist.*, xxx (1979), pp 1–28.

10. Citations in Edwards, *Church and state*, pp 139, 140.

11. See especially the work of A. Clarke, *The Old English in Ireland 1625–42* (London, 1966) and in *N.H.I.*, iii, 187–288; H. F. Kearney, *Strafford in Ireland 1633–41* (Manchester, 1959).

12. On the continental seminaries see J. Brady, 'The Irish colleges in Europe and the Counter-reformation' in *Ir. Cath. Hist. Comm. Proc.* (1957), pp 1–8; 'Father Christopher Cusack and the Irish college at Douai' in *Measgra Mhichíl Uí Chléirigh*, pp 98–117; H. Hammerstein, 'Aspects of the continental education of Irish students in the reign of Elizabeth I' in *Hist. Studies*, viii, 137–54; T. J. Walsh, *The Irish continental college movement* (Dublin, 1973). The 1622 list of Douai alumni is in J. Brady (ed.), 'The Irish Colleges in the Low Countries' in *Archiv. Hib.*, xiv (1949), pp 66–91 and the Salamanca admission oaths are in D. J. O'Doherty (ed.), 'Students of the Irish College, Salamanca', ibid., ii (1913), pp 1–36, iii (1914), pp 87–112. For Irish students of Louvain see B. Jennings (ed.), 'Irish students in the university of Louvain' in *Measgra Mhichíl Uí Chléirigh*, pp

74–97. For the Jesuits see especially E. Hogan, *Ibernia Ignatiana* (Dublin, 1890) and *Distinguished Irishmen of the sixteenth century* (London, 1894). For the Franciscans see C. Mooney, 'The golden age of the Irish Franciscans' in *Measgra Mhichíl Uí Chléirigh,* pp 21–33.

13. C. Giblin, 'The "Processus Datariae" and the appointment of Irish bishops in the seventeenth century' in *Father Luke Wadding,* pp 524, 542–4.

14. I have studied these issues in some detail in 'An Irish Counter-reformation bishop: John Roche' in *Ir. Theol. Quart.,* xxv (1958), pp 14–32, 101–23, xxvi (1959), pp 101–16, 313–30.

15. The two most useful sources are synodal decrees and episcopal reports on their dioceses. The principal synods are: Drogheda (1614) in Renehan, *Collections,* i, 116–46, 427–37; Kilkenny (1614) in P. F. Moran, *History of the Catholic archbishops of Dublin* (Dublin, 1864), pp 440–63; Armagh province (1618), ibid., pp 427–31; Cashel province (1624) in *Wadding papers,* pp 83–8; Tuam province (1631 and 1639–40), in Renehan, *Collections,* i, 491–9. The principal reports are in *Archiv. Hib.,* iii (1914), pp 359–65 (Elphin, 1631), and v (1916), pp 75–118 (Dublin, 1619; Kilmore, 1629; Kilmore, 1634; Ossory, 1635; Ferns, 1635; Elphin, 1637; Tuam, 1637; Kildare, 1637; Down and Connor, 1639; Waterford, 1639; Dublin, 1641; Limerick, 1649).

Ecclesiastical correspondence is in general disappointing. It tends to concentrate on clerical problems, but there are also accounts of religious developments. Special mention might be made of Moran, *Spicil. Ossor.,* i and *Wadding papers.* There is much material from Propaganda archives in *Archiv. Hib.* and *Collect. Hib.:* see especially B. Jennings (ed.), 'Acta sacrae congregationis de Propaganda Fide 1622–1650' in *Archiv. Hib.,* xxii (1959), pp 28–139.

Material will be found scattered through *Cal. S.P.Ire.* and *Cal. Carew MSS.* The visitations mentioned in note 8 above can be useful. Archbishop Bulkeley's visitation of Dublin in 1630 (ed. M. V. Ronan in *Archiv. Hib.,* vii (1941), pp. 36–98) gives the most detailed factual account of Catholicism in the diocese at the time.

16. *Wadding papers,* p. 609.

17. See Herbert Wood, 'The Court of Castle Chamber' in *R.I.A. Proc.,* xxxii (1913–16), sect. C, pp 152–70. The records of the court down to 1620 are in *H.M.C. Egmont MSS,* i, pt 1 (1905), pp. 1–60. For Francis Taylor see Joannes Molanus, *Idea togatae constantiae . . .* (Paris, 1629). See also the long report by Archbishop Lombard (c. 1617) ed. J. Hagan, 'Miscellanea Vaticano-Hibernica, 1580–1631' in *Archiv. Hib.,* iii (1914), pp 324–59; R. Walsh (ed.), 'Persecution of Catholics in Drogheda in 1606, 1607 and 1611', ibid., vi (1917), pp 64–8; J. Meagher, 'Presentments of recusants in Dublin 1617–1618' in *Reportorium Novum,* ii, 2 (1959–60), pp 269–73.

18. *Comment. Rinucc.,* v, 151–7.

19. In Hore, *Wexford,* vi, 259.

20. For a general survey see B. Ó Cuív, 'The Irish language in the early modern period' in *N.H.I.,* iii, 509–45.

21. For the chapels in Derry see W. P. Burke (ed.), 'The diocese of Derry in 1631' in *Archiv. Hib.,* v (1916), pp 1–6. Brereton's account of his travels in 1635 is printed in Falkiner, *Illustrations,* pp 363–407. The description of the Jesuit chapel in Dublin is at p. 382.

22. Calendared by B. Millett in *Collect. Hib.*, vi–vii (1963–4), pp 46–50.
23. Moran, *Spicil. Ossor.*, i, 115–19.
24. R. J. Hunter (ed.), 'Catholicism in Meath, c. 1622' in *Collect. Hib.*, xiv (1971),' p. 9; H. Piers, 'A chorographical description of the county of West-Meath, written A.D. 1682' in C. Vallancey, *Collectanea de rebus Hibernicis,* i (Dublin, 1770), pp 63–4; Lodge, *Peerage Ire.* (ed. M. Archdall, Dublin, 1789), i, 243.
25. Moran, *Spicil. Ossor.*, ii, 50–51.
26. Hunter, art. cit., p. 9. For Drogheda see *Wadding papers*, pp 39–40, 639.
27. Bossy, art. cit., p. 166; Clarke, art. cit., p. 70.
28. *Wadding papers*, p. 544.
29. E. Hogan (ed.), *Ibernia Ignatiana* (Dublin, 1890), p. 161.
30. A. Hutton (tr.), *The Embassy in Ireland of Monsignor G. B. Rinuccini* (Dublin, 1873), pp 141–4.
31. Bossy, art. cit., p. 169.

Chapter 3 (pp 43–72)

1. I have treated the confederate Catholics at some length in *The origins of Catholic Nationalism* (Dublin, 1968) and in *N.H.I.*, iii, 289–335.
2. *The Unkinde Desertor* (Ghent, 1676), p. 13.
3. See my survey in *N.H.I.*, iii, 336–86; T. C. Barnard, *Cromwellian Ireland* (Oxford, 1976); St John D. Seymour, *The Puritans in Ireland* (Oxford, 1912).
4. *Writings*, ed. Abbott, ii, 146.
5. Op. cit., p. 172.
6. Documentation in Comerford, *Kildare and Leighlin*, i, 320–23.
7. See especially T. C. Barnard, 'Planters and policies in Cromwellian Ireland' in *Past & Present*, no. 61 (Nov. 1973), pp 31–69.
8. T. O'Fiaich, 'Edmund O'Reilly, archbishop of Armagh, 1657–1669' in *Father Luke Wadding*, pp 171–228; B. Millett, 'Archbishop Edmund O'Reilly's report on the state of the Church in Ireland in 1662' in *Collect. Hib.*, ii (1959), pp 105–14.
9. Renehan, *Collections*, i, 499–506 (Tuam); *Comment. Rinucc.*, v, 391–6 (Armagh); B. Millett (ed.), in *Archiv. Hib.*, xxviii (1966), pp 45–52 (Cashel).
10. St John D. Seymour, op. cit., pp 92–4.
11. R. Clark, *Strangers and sojourners at Port Royal* (Cambridge, 1932), pp 187–219.
12. Useful studies of the Restoration period are J. G. Simms in *N.H.I.*, iii, 420–53 (political and general); B. Millett, *Survival and Reorganisation 1650–95* (Dublin, 1968 – religious) and E. MacLysaght, *Irish life in the seventeenth century: after Cromwell* (ed. 2, Cork, 1950 – social).
13. *N.H.I.*, iii, 386, 427.
14. See note 18 below.
15. J. Hanly (ed.), *The Letters of Saint Oliver Plunkett* (Dublin, 1979), p. 574.
16. Ibid., p. 151.
17. In B. Millett (ed.), 'Calendar of volume I of the *Scritture riferite nei congressi, Irlanda* in Propaganda archives' in *Collect. Hib.*, vi–vii (1963–4), pp 144–8.
18. For the areas for which material was collected see the map in *N.H.I.*, iii, 456. For those printed, see H. F. Hore, 'Particulars relative to Wexford and the barony of Forth, by Colonel Solomon Richards, 1682' in *R.S.A.I.Jn*, vii

(1862–3), pp 84–92; 'A chorographic account of the southern part of County Wexford, written anno 1684, by Robert Leigh, esq., of Rosegarland in that county', ibid., v (1858–9), pp 17–21, 451–67; 'An account of the barony of Forth in the County of Wexford, written at the close of the seventeenth century', ibid, vii (1862–3), pp 53–83; W. O'Sullivan (ed.), 'William Molyneux's geographical collections for Kerry' in *Kerry Arch. Soc. Jn.*, iv (1971), pp 28–47; Roderick O'Flaherty, *A chorographical description of West or h-Iar Connaught, written A.D. 1684*, ed. J. Hardiman (Dublin, 1846); Henry Piers, 'A chorographical description of the County of West-Meath, written A.D. 1682' in C. Vallancey, *Collectanea de rebus Hibernicis*, i, (Dublin, 1770), 1–126; S. P. Johnston (ed.), 'On a manuscript description of the city and county of Cork, circa 1685, written by Sir Richard Cox' in *R.S.A.I.Jn.*, xxxii (1902), pp 353–76; 'Co. Kildare in 1683' in MacLysaght, *Ir. life after Cromwell*, pp 313–19.

19. I have edited the 'Notebook' in *Archiv. Hib.*, xxix (1970), pp 49–114. His letter to Propaganda is in Moran, *Spicil. Ossor.*, ii, 264–5.

20. Bishop Phelan's will was edited by W. Carrigan in *Archiv. Hib.*, iv (1915), pp 85–8. His account of his diocese in 1678 is in Moran, *Spicil. Ossor.*, ii, 253–4 and his diocesan regulations for 1672 and 1676 ibid., iii, 92–102.

21. Bishop Brenan's correspondence is in P. Power, *A bishop of the Penal times* (Cork, 1932), and his diocesan regulations for 1672 and 1676 are in Moran, *Spicil. Ossor.*, ii, 226–42.

22. Ed. John Hanly, *The letters of St Oliver Plunkett* (Dublin, 1979). Despite its curious arrangement and faults of omission, P. F. Moran, *Memoir of Oliver Plunket* (ed. 2, Dublin, 1895) has not been completely supplanted, though there are quite a number of recent studies on particular points, especially in *Seanchas Ardmhacha*. Among them might be noted T. O'Fiaich, 'The fall and return of John McMoyer' (iii, 1 (1958), pp 51–86).

23. In Moran, *Spicil. Ossor.*, iii, 117–26.

24. The Armagh decrees of 1670 are in Renehan, *Collections*, i, 151–5 and Moran, *Memoir of Oliver Plunket*, pp 146–9; the Armagh decrees of 1678 are ibid., pp 150–56. For the Kilmore synod of 1687 see Moran, *Spicil. Ossor.*, iii, 109–15. I have been unable to find any information on the word *gierador*. The copy of these decrees from which Moran printed his text is in the Dublin diocesan archives. It may be of the early eighteenth century. One gets a distinct impression that the writer, who wrote a very elegant hand, did not know Irish at all and was simply trying to reproduce mechanically the shape of the letters in the word in Irish in his exemplar.

25. John Lynch, *Alithinologia* (St Malo, 1664), p. 136; Nicholas French, *The Unkinde Desertor* (Ghent, 1676), p. 6.

26. Edward MacLysaght (ed.), *The Kenmare Manuscripts* (Dublin, 1942), p. 271; P. S. Dinneen and Tadhg O'Donoghue (eds.), *The Poems of Egan O'Rahilly* (ed. 2, London, 1911), pp 116–17:

    I will follow the beloved among heroes to the grave,
    Those princes my fathers served before the death of Christ.

27. For Thomas Dineley see E. P. Shirley (ed.), 'Extracts from the Journal of Thomas Dineley' in *R.S.A.I.Jn.*, iv (1856–7) to ix (1867). Long extracts from Dunton's letters are printed in MacLysaght, *Ir. life after Cromwell*, pp 320–90.

28. *The Political Anatomy of Ireland* (London, 1691, reprinted Shannon, 1970), p. 96.

Chapter 4 (pp 73–81)

There is still no fully satisfactory study of the Penal Code. Apart from the general histories of the eighteenth century, still overshadowed by Lecky's great work, Maureen Wall, *The Penal Laws 1691–1760* (Dundalk, 1961) and John Brady and Patrick J. Corish, *The Church under the Penal Code* (Dublin, 1971) may be consulted. J. G. Simms, 'The making of a penal law, 1703–4' in *I.H.S.*, xii (Sept. 1960), pp 105–18 gives valuable detailed information on how one of the most far-reaching of the penal statutes came to be passed. The contributions of Thomas Arkins, 'The commercial aspects of the Penal Code' and 'The Penal Laws and Irish land' (*Studies*, i (1912), pp 257–73, 514–23) are still worth consulting.

1. H. Fenning (ed.), 'Some eighteenth-century broadsheets' in *Collect. Hib.*, xii (1969), p. 52.
2. Burke, *Penal times*, p. 236.
3. Brady, *Eighteenth-century press*, pp 15–16.
4. *The History of England* (ed. and abridged with an introduction by Hugh Trevor-Roper (Penguin Books, 1979), p. 353.
5. *The Humble Address of John Whaley to the Lords Spiritual, Temporal and Commons.*
6. Brady, *Eighteenth-century press*, p. 60.
7. Church organsiation is treated more fully in J. Brady and P. J. Corish, *The Church under the Penal Code* (Dublin, 1971), pp 26–49.

Chapter 5 (pp 82–114)

In addition to *Archivium Hibernicum, Collectanea Hibernica* and *Spicilegium Ossoriense*, W. P. Burke, *The Irish Priests in the Penal Times* (Waterford, 1914 – Public Record Office documentation since lost) and John Brady, *Catholics and Catholicism in the eighteenth-century Press* (Maynooth, 1965) provide valuable source-material.

1. M. Wall, 'The Catholics of the towns and the quarterage dispute in eighteenth-century Ireland' in *I.H.S.*, viii (Sept. 1952), pp 91–114; 'The rise of a Catholic middle class in eighteenth-century Ireland', ibid., xi (Sept. 1958), pp 91–115.
2. N. Burke, 'A hidden Church?: the structure of Catholic Dublin in the mid-eighteenth century' in *Archiv. Hib.*, xxxii (1974), pp 81–92.
3. Archbishop Byrne's regulations are in Moran, *Spicil. Ossor.*, iii, 128–9 and the 1730 statutes ibid., pp 139–48.
4. W. Carrigan edited from the Public Record Office 'Catholic episcopal wills' (*Archiv. Hib.*, i (1912), pp 148–200, ii (1913), pp 220–41, iii (1914), pp 160–202, iv (1915), pp 66–95). They do not contain much relevant to the present investigation. This item of information is in *Archiv. Hib.*, iv, 72.
5. The information that follows is drawn mainly from H. Fenning (ed.), 'Letters from a Jesuit in Dublin on the Confraternity of the Holy Name, 1747–1748' in *Archiv. Hib.*, xxix (1970), pp 133–54 and his study of the Irish Dominican province between 1698 and 1761 in *Archivum Fratrum Praedicatorum,* xxxviii (1968), pp 259–357, xlii (1972), pp 252–368, xlv (1975), pp 399–502.
6. There are a number of useful studies in *Reportorium Novum*, the Dublin diocesan historical journal: T. Wall, 'Archbishop Carpenter and the Catholic revival, 1770–1786' (i, 1 (1955), pp 173–82); W. Hawkes, 'Irish form of

preparation for Sunday Mass in the eighteenth century' (ibid., pp 183–92); J. Brady, 'Catholic schools in Dublin in 1787–8' (ibid., pp 193–6); M. J. Curran (ed.), 'Archbishop Carpenter's Epistolae (1770–1780)' (ibid., pp 154–72, continued in i, 2 (1956), pp 381–98) and 'Instructions, admonitions etc. of Archbishop Carpenter, 1770–1786' (ii, 1 (1957–8), pp 148–71); J. Meagher, 'Glimpses of eighteenth-century Dublin priests' (ii, 1 (1957–8), pp 130–47).

7. T. Wall, *The Sign of Dr Hay's Head* (Dublin, 1958) is, as its sub-title indicates, 'some account of the hazards and fortunes of Catholic printers and publishers in Dublin from later penal times to the present day'.

8. R. Clark, *Strangers and sojourners at Port Royal* (Cambridge, 1932), pp 204–19.

9. An account of John Donnelly's library is given by Hugh Fenning in *Collect Hib.*, xviii–xix (1976–7), pp 72–104, and of John Wickham's by P. O Súilleabháin, ibid., vi–vii (1963–4), pp 234–44.

10. P. O Súilleabháin, 'Documents relating to Wexford friary and parish, 1733–98' in *Collect. Hib.*, viii (1965), pp 110–28.

11. Moran, *Spicil. Ossor.*, ii, 395–8.

12. M. Wall, *The Penal Laws 1691–1760*, p. 53.

13. Burke, *Penal times*, p. 419.

14. J. G. Simms, 'Connacht in the eighteenth century' in *I.H.S.*, xi (Sept. 1958), pp 116–33 is an excellent survey.

15. Liam Swords, 'Calendar of the papers of the Irish College, Paris' in *Archiv. Hib.*, xxxv (1980), pp 95, 103.

16. Burke, *Penal times*, pp 412–53; *Archiv. Hib.*, iii (1914), pp 124–59.

17. *Collect. Hib.*, v (1962), pp 9–10.

18. The Achonry statutes are in Moran, *Spicil. Ossor.*, iii, 272–3; the 1753 report on Elphin is in *Archiv. Hib.*, xxx (1972), pp 21–8; that of 1770 with those for Tuam and Killala ibid., v (1916), pp 143–56. For the letters see H. Fenning (ed.), 'The journey of James Lyons from Rome to Sligo, 1763–65' in *Collect. Hib.*, xi (1968), pp 91–110.

19. Thomas Mahon, O.F.M. See C. Giblin, 'Ten documents relating to Irish diocesan affairs 1740–84, from Franciscan Library, Killiney' in *Collect. Hib.*, xx (1978), pp 55–88, at pp 73–5.

20. The Ulster material is on pp 267–96.

21. P. O Maolagáin (ed.), 'An early History of Fermanagh' in *Clogher Rec.*, i, 4 (1956), ii, 1 (1957), ii, 2 (1958), ii, 3 (1959). The passage cited is at i, 4 (1956), pp 113–14.

22. Printed in Moran, *Spicil. Ossor.*, ii, 470–89. For an English translation see P. J. Flanagan (ed.), 'The diocese of Clogher in 1714' in *Clogher Rec.*, i, 39–43, 125–30 (1954, 1955). See also L. J. Flynn, 'Archbishop Hugh MacMahon' in *Seanchas Ardmhacha*, vii, 1 (1973), pp 108–75.

23. In *Archiv. Hib.*, i (1912), pp 10–27.

24. In *Archiv. Hib.*, v (1916), pp 132–4, Renehan, *Collections*, i, 104–5 and *Archiv. Hib.*, xii (1946), pp 62–9 respectively.

25. Brady, *Eighteenth-century press*, p.225. Many other examples are recorded.

26. L. M. Cullen, 'The Hidden Ireland: reassessment of a concept' in *Studia Hib.*, ix (1969), pp 7–47. See also S. Ó Tuama, 'Donall Ó Corcora' in *Scríobh*, iv (1979), pp 94–108; B. Ó Buachalla, 'Ó Corcora agus an Hidden Ireland', ibid., pp 109–37.

27. *A Tour in Ireland 1776–1779* (Shannon, 1970), i, 300.
28. Burke, *Penal times*, pp 297–411. See also Brady, *Eighteenth-century press.*
29. Burke, *Penal times*, p. 389.
30. *Archiv. Hib.*, ii (1913), pp 108–56 (Cashel); iv (1915), pp 131–77 (Dublin).
31. Ferns statutes for 1722 in *Archiv. Hib.*, xxvii (1964), pp 76–84; Dublin for 1730 in Moran, *Spicil. Ossor.*, iii, 139–47; and Cashel for 1737 in Renehan, *Collections*, i, 465–7.
32. The principal documents, listed in chronological order, are: Martin Marley, *The Good Confessor* (Douai, 1943); diocesan regulations for Kildare and Leighlin (1748) in Comerford, *Kildare and Leighlin*, i, 78–82 and for Ossory (1748) in Carrigan, *Ossory*, i, 152–3; visitation of Ferns (1753) in *Archiv. Hib.*, ii (1913), pp 100–105; visitations of Cashel, mostly in the 1750s, in *Archiv. Hib.*, xxxiii (1975), pp 1–90, xxxiv (1976–7), pp 1–49; the 'Constitutio Apostolica' of Bishop Madgett of Kerry (c. 1760) in *Kerry Arch. Soc. Jn.*, ix (1976), pp 68–91; diocesan statutes of Cashel (1763) in Renehan, *Collections*, i, 471–3; diocesan report on Ossory (1769) in *Archiv. Hib.*, v (1916), pp 135–42; diocesan regulations for Ferns (1771) in *Archiv. Hib.*, iii (1914), pp 113–23; report on the dioceses of Cloyne and Ross (1775) in Moran, *Spicil. Ossor.*, iii, 338–41; material relating to Ossory from Bishop Troy's correspondence (1776–86) in Moran, *Spicil. Ossor.*, iii, 361–84; diocesan report on Dublin (1780) in *Reportorium Novum*, i, 2 (1956), pp 392–8; Bishop Plunkett's visitations in Cogan, *Meath, passim*, but especially those of 1780 (iii, 25–44); Cashel statutes (1782) in Renehan, *Collections*, i, 473–9; diocesan report on Kerry (1785) in *Kerry Arch. Soc. Jn.*, vii (1974), pp 21–36; diocesan report on Ferns (1796) in *Archiv. Hib.*, xxviii (1966), pp 103–113; diocesan report on Dublin (1802) in Moran, *Spicil. Ossor.*, iii, 625–46.
33. *Archiv. Hib.*, ii (1913), p. 103.
34. Brady, *Eighteenth-century press*, p. 246.
35. T. P. Cunningham, 'The 1766 religious census, Kilmore and Ardagh' in *Breifne*, i, 4 (1961), pp 357–62.
36. *The speeches of John Philpot Curran*, pp xvi–xvii.
37. *Archiv. Hib.*, i (1912), p. 225.
38. E. Larkin, 'The devotional revolution in Ireland, 1850–75' in *A.H.R.*, lxxvii (1972), pp 625–52; D. Miller, 'Irish Catholicism and the great Famine' in *Journal of Social History*, ix (1975), pp 81–98.
39. Brady, *Eighteenth-century press*, pp 232–48.
40. Ibid., p. 265.
41. The bishop frequently speaks of this problem. The two instances cited are from Cogan, *Meath*, iii, 33, 34.
42. Brady, *Eighteenth-century press*, p. 73.
43. There is a good summary by Michael Tynan, 'The end of an era' in *The Furrow*, xxv (1974), pp 660–71.
44. Here much remains to be done. See R. A. Breatnach, 'The end of a tradition' in *Studia. Hib.*, i (1961), pp 128–50; T. Ó Fiaich, 'The language and political history' in B. Ó Cuiv (ed.), *A view of the Irish language* (Dublin, 1969), pp 101–11; 'Irish poetry and the clergy' in *Léachtaí Cholm Cille*, iv (Maynooth, 1975), pp 30–56; M. Wall, 'The decline of the Irish language' in B. Ó Cuiv, op. cit., pp 81–90.
45. Cogan, *Meath*, iii, 30.

46. Comerford, *Kildare and Leighlin*, i, 81.
47. *Archiv. Hib.*, iii (1914), p. 117.
48. *The Good Confessor*, p. 73.
49. *Archiv. Hib.*, v (1916), p. 154.
50. Moran, *Spicil. Ossor.*, iii, 578.
51. *Archiv. Hib.*, iii (1914), p. 118; Moran, *Spicil. Ossor.*, iii, 379.
52. *The Banks of the Boro* (London and Dublin, 1867), pp 60–62.

Chapter 6 (pp 115–144)
Among the general histories of the eighteenth century, W. E. H. Lecky, *History of Ireland in the Eighteenth Century* (5 vols., London, 1892) is still indispensable, especially for its extensive citations, though he was not primarily interested in the line of investigation pursued here. J. A. Froude, *The English in Ireland in the Eighteenth Century* (3 vols., London, 1882) has its uses as a quarry. Among more modern works might be mentioned Francis Goodwin James, *Ireland in the Empire 1688–1770* (Harvard, 1973) and E. M. Johnston, *Ireland in the Eighteenth Century* (Dublin, 1974).

1. Brady, *Eighteenth-century press*, pp 70–71.
2. McDowell, *Ir. public opinion*, p. 10.
3. The point is sensitively made by Frank O'Connor, *The Backward Look* (London, 1967), pp 115–16.
4. George Marlay, bishop of Dromore (Brady, *Eighteenth-century press*, p. 68).
5. For an excellent summary see M. Wall, 'Catholic loyalty to king and pope in eighteenth-century Ireland' in *Ir. Cath. Hist. Comm. Proc.* (1961), pp 17–24.
6. *A Tour in Ireland 1776–1779* (Shannon, 1970), ii, 53–4.
7. E. MacLysaght (ed.), *The Kenmare Manuscripts* (Dublin, 1942). A number of examples are assembled by S. Ó Tuama, 'Donall Ó Corcora' in *Scríobh*, iv (1979), pp 104–5.
8. See especially M. Wall, 'The Whiteboys' in T. D. Williams (ed.), *Secret Societies in Ireland* (Dublin, 1973), pp 13–25; J. S. Donnelly, 'The Whiteboy movement, 1761–5' in *I.H.S.*, xxi (March 1978), pp 20–54.
9. Brady, *Eighteenth-century press*, p. 110.
10. *An Historical and Critical Review of the Civil Wars in Ireland* (Dublin, 1786), ii, 274.
11. Brady, *Eighteenth-century press*, p. 140.
12. Lecky, *Ire.*, i, 167.
13. Quoted ibid., ii, 23. A friend has called my attention to a poem in R. I. A. MS 23 E 12, pp 409–10, entitled 'Clann Shádhbha agas Sháidhbhin: a Whiteboy song'. The scribe is Nioclás Ó Cearnaigh (d. 1846). He gives no author, but the text would suggest a southern origin and a date possibly about the time of the Whiteboy disturbances. The poem lists 'Sádhbh' among the fairy queens: 'Aoibheal, Áine, Sádhbh a's Gráinne'.
14. See R. A. Breatnach, 'The lady and the king: a theme of Irish literature' in *Studies*, xlii (1953), pp 321–36.
15. Art. cit., p. 40.
16. Brady, *Eighteenth-century press*, p.115.
17. Quoted in Lecky, *Ire.*, ii, 37.
18. M. J. Curran (ed.), 'Instructions, admonitions etc. of Archbishop Carpenter' in *Reportorium Novum*, ii, 1 (1957–8), pp 148–67.

19. *A Tour in Ireland 1776–1779* (Shannon, 1970), ii, 214.
20. Quoted in Froude, *Ire.*, ii, 132–3.
21. J. S. Donnelly, 'The Rightboy movement' in *Studia Hib.*, xvii–xviii (1977–8), pp 120–202.
22. Brady, *Eighteenth-century press*, pp 232–46; Carrigan, *Ossory*, i, 193–4.
23. Donnelly, art. cit., p. 181. In the following five pages he tries to quantify the general level of Rightboy violence.
24. A. Houston (ed.), *Daniel O'Connell: his early life and Journal, 1795 to 1802* (London, 1906), p. 155.
25. See the interesting study by Marianne Elliott, 'The origins and transformation of early Irish republicanism' in *International Review of Social History* [Amsterdam], xxiii (1978), pp 405–28.
26. The opening chapters of Hereward Senior, *Orangeism in Ireland and Britain 1795–1836* (London, 1966) are useful.
27. Thomas Pakenham, *The Year of Liberty* (London, 1972), p. 39.
28. *Irish land and British politics: tenant-right and nationality 1865–1870* (Cambridge, 1974).
29. Barbara Solow, *The land question and the Irish economy 1870–1903* (Harvard, 1971), pp 203–4.

Index